This book belongs to:

....

It was given to me by:

....

On:

....

3-Minute
Bedtime Devotions
for
Little Hearts

3-Minute
Bedtime Devotions
for
Little Hearts

Rae Simons

BARBOUR
kidz
A Division of Barbour Publishing

© 2023 by Barbour Publishing, Inc.

Print ISBN 978-1-63609-510-3

Scripture quotations are taken from the New Life Version copyright © 1969 and 2003 by Barbour Publishing, Inc., Uhrichsville, Ohio, 44683. All rights reserved.

Published by Barbour Publishing, Inc., 1810 Barbour Drive, Uhrichsville, Ohio 44683

Our mission is to inspire the world with the life-changing message of the Bible.

Member of the
Evangelical Christian
Publishers Association

Printed in China.

001485 0223   DS

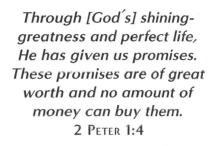

Through [God's] shining-
greatness and perfect life,
He has given us promises.
These promises are of great
worth and no amount of
money can buy them.
2 PETER 1:4

Introduction

Bedtime is a good time to think about God. It's a good time to get to know Him a little better by spending time with Him. As you read this book, you'll have a chance to read a verse from the Bible. Then you'll get some ideas for how to think about that verse. You'll see how the verse has a message to you from God. Finally, this book will help you start talking to God. You can begin with the prayer on each page—but then keep going. Tell God all about your thoughts and feelings. Tell Him what happened to you today. God loves you, and He wants you to share everything with Him!

When No One Answers

*"Ask, and what you are asking
for will be given to you."*
MATTHEW 7:7

Do you ever feel mad when you ask a question and no one answers? Jesus was a human being just like you. He knows what it's like to be a kid. He understands that it's easy to get tired of waiting for grown-ups to answer you when you ask a question. In this Bible verse, Jesus promises you that God hears when you ask a question. Sometimes, though, it might seem like you've been asking and asking, and God just never answers. But don't give up. Don't stop asking questions. God loves to hear your voice! He will never get impatient with you.

● ●

Jesus, thank You that I can ask You anything.

God Never Forgets

But Zion said, "The Lord has left me
alone. The Lord has forgotten me."
Isaiah **49:14**

Do you ever wonder if God has forgotten you? Maybe you
got in trouble at school. Maybe you and your best friend
had a fight. Maybe your parents yelled at you. Or maybe
all those things happened on the same day! *God doesn't
really care about me,* you think. *If He did, He wouldn't let so
many bad things happen.* But God doesn't ever leave you.
Sometimes you may not be able to tell He is there—but He
is! Even if you can't feel His love for a little while, He never
stops loving you, and He never forgets you.

. . . .

Thank You, Father God,
for always being with me.

You Can Help People See Jesus

*[Jesus said,] "Whoever receives one of these
little children in My name, receives Me."*
MARK 9:37

People sometimes describe God as an old man with a long
white beard. But the Bible never says God looks like an old
man. In fact, Jesus says just the opposite. He says that He
is like a child! He means that children can help grown-ups
see and understand God better. When you show love to your
family, you are showing them Jesus. When you are kind to
someone, you help them know God loves them. You are an
important part of what God is doing in the world!

. . . .

*Thank You, Jesus, that I can show You to
other people. Help me never to forget what
an important job You've given me.*

Hope in God

Hope in the Lord!
PSALM 130:7

The Bible says you don't have to worry that God is mad
at you. God always loves you, no matter what. So you can
always "hope" in God. When the Bible talks about hope, it
doesn't mean wishing. When you wish for something, you
might get what you want, or you might not. But the Bible's
hope means that even if you can't understand God, you know
He loves you. You don't know what will happen tomorrow or
next week or next year—but you know God loves you. You
might feel mixed up and worried—but you know God loves
you! That's what it means to hope in God.

• •

Thank You, Father God,
that You always love me.

David's God-Rock

*"The Lord is my rock, my strong place,
and the One Who sets me free."*

2 SAMUEL 22:2

The person who wrote these words was a man named David. David and God were close friends, and God did a lot of wonderful things for David. But David also made mistakes. As soon as David said he was sorry, though, God was ready to forgive him. David knew he could count on God. So when something scary happened, David ran to God. When David got in trouble, he asked God to help him. God was like a big rock, a place where David could climb to the top and be safe.

* *

*Lord God, I want You to be my rock
the way You were for David.*

Saved!

"God saves me. I will trust and not be afraid."
ISAIAH 12:2

Do you understand what being "saved" means? Sometimes people think it means we'll go to heaven when we die. This is true —but being saved is also something that happens right now. It means that when you give yourself to God, He washes you clean and makes you healthy on the inside. He cares about everything that happens to you, even the teeny-tiny things. He is helping you to grow strong and learn new things. And He is always right there, ready to help you.

• •

Lord God, I'm sorry for all the times I mess up. I want You to save me tonight— and every day, for the rest of my life.

Happy!

Then Hannah prayed and said,
"My heart is happy in the Lord."
1 Samuel 2:1

Your prayers might sound something like this: *Father God, please help my grandma to feel better. Help my brother and me not to fight so much. Help my mother and father not to argue.* These are all good things to pray, because God wants to know the things that are worrying you. He wants you to pray about all those things. He wants to help you with all the things that are hard in your life. But He also wants you to talk to Him even when you don't need anything. He wants you to tell Him about the things that make you happy. He loves to be happy with you!

• •

Father God, thank You for all the
happy times I had today.

Get Your Head off the Pillow

But You, O Lord, are. . .the
One Who lifts my head.
PSALM 3:3

Do you ever feel like pulling the covers over your head in
the morning? You just don't want to get up and do all the
things you're supposed to do—like getting dressed, eating
breakfast, going to school. . . You'd rather stay home and
play. A man named David in the Bible had those feelings too.
When he wrote this psalm, he was in big trouble—even the
people he loved most were mad at him. But David knew God
would help him lift his head off the pillow and get going.

. . . .

Lord God, if tomorrow is one of those
days when I don't feel like getting
up, I know You will help me.

Little Things

Jesus said, "Let her alone. Why are you giving her trouble? She has done a good thing to Me. . . . She did what she could."
MARK 14:6, 8

Do you ever think there's not much you can do for God because you're just a kid? If you ever feel like that, Jesus has a message He wants you to hear. He wants you to do whatever you can for Him now—even if it's something that seems very little. Sometimes very little things can make a *big* difference! Your smile could make someone feel a little happier. Your kind words might help someone understand that God loves them. When you do even little things for others, you are showing God that you love Him!

• •

When I get up tomorrow, remind me, Father God, to find little things I can do for others and for You.

The Fire of God

For our God is a fire that destroys everything.
HEBREWS **12:29**

This verse says that God is a fire. It means that God's love is *like* a fire. It burns up everything that's bad, leaving only the good things behind. If you're feeling selfish, God's love wants to burn up that feeling! If you're selfish—if you always want your own way, if you want the biggest and best things, if you want to be first and always win every game—well, then love doesn't have much room to live inside you. It's not easy to let our selfishness get burned up. But it's worth it. Only love makes us *really* happy.

. . . .

Lord God, go ahead—burn up my selfishness with Your cleansing fire.

Life Giver

Then they may know that You alone,
Whose name is the Lord, are the
Most High over all the earth.
PSALM **83:18**

A long time ago, *lords* were the people in charge of every-thing. They were the ones who could tell other people what to do. So when we call God "Lord," we are saying He's in charge. He can tell us what to do, and we'll do it. But when David, the man who wrote this verse, used the word *Lord*, it meant "Life Giver"—the one who gives life to you and me and everything in the world. God rules the world with love. He wants to be in charge of your life—not because He's bossy, but because He always wants what is best for you!

. . . .

Father God, thank You that You
always know what's best for me.

Sunshine in the Dark

*Light is pleasing. It is good for
the eyes to see the sun.*
ECCLESIASTES 11:7

Do you like sunny days or gray days better? Almost every-one likes sunny days. Sunny days make us feel happy. They remind us that even if bad things happen sometimes, the world is a beautiful place. And God wants to share those happy feelings with you. He loves to see you smile and laugh. He smiles too when He sees you playing and having a good time. He's right there with you, and He wants to be part of your good times. Let Him play and laugh and smile with you.

. . . .

*God of sunshine, tomorrow when I laugh and
smile and play, remind me to think of You.*

Girls and Boys

In the likeness of God He made him.
He made both male and female.
GENESIS 1:27

God made girls and boys. The Bible says that if you're a girl, you're like God! And if you're a boy, you're like God too! Boys aren't better than girls, and girls aren't better than boys. Boys and girls are different from each other in some ways, but they are both made to be like God. The same goes for women and men. The women in your life who love you can help you understand God's love a little better, because God loves you like a mother does. And the men in your life who love you can teach you about God as well, because God loves you like a father.

* *

Lord God, thank You for making me like You!

Friends

*Jonathan went to David. . .and
gave him strength in God.*
1 Samuel 23:16

Do you have a best friend? David had a best friend named
Jonathan. David and Jonathan loved each other and talked
to each other. When one of them was in trouble, the other
one did whatever he could to help. Jonathan's friendship
helped David be strong in God. You too can see God in your
friends. When a friend smiles at you or listens to you, God
is using that friend to show you how much He loves you.
It works the other way too. When you are kind to a friend,
you help them know God loves them. Friends help us grow
and understand God better.

* *

*Thank You, Father God, for my friends. I want to
help them see You and know that You love them.*

Loving-Kindness

The loving-kindness of God lasts all day long.
PSALM 52:1

When something bad happens, do you ever wonder if God is *really* loving and kind? When a pet dies, that doesn't seem very loving or kind, does it? Or if a friend moves away or a grandparent is sick, those don't seem like kind and loving things either. So how could our friend David (who wrote this verse) say that God's loving-kindness lasts all day? David knew that bad things happen in life. When we feel unhappy and hurt, it's hard to believe God's love is real. But God's love isn't about how we feel. He never promised to keep all bad things from happening. But when bad things happen, His love is there to help.

• •

*Lord God, when bad things happen, help
me remember that You still love me.*

Faith in God

Jesus said to [His followers],
"Have faith in God."
MARK 11:22

Do you know what it means to have faith in God? Faith doesn't mean you never make mistakes. It doesn't mean you're always happy or good or kind. Faith *is* about what God is like. So when you have faith *in God,* even when you mess up, God will forgive you and help you do better next time. When you have faith in God, you know He's still with you even when you're sad or afraid. If you feel like you don't have a lot of faith yet, that's okay. Faith isn't something you make—it's something God gives you. The more time you spend with God, the more faith you will have!

. . . .

Father God, I want to have more faith in
You. Teach me what I need to learn.

Serving God

"Serve the Lord your God."
EXODUS 23:25

Can you think of ways to serve God? If you were to make a list, you might say things like going to church, praying, and reading the Bible. Those are all good ways to serve God. But the Bible says the best way to serve God is to love Him and to love other people. This means that serving God isn't something we do just on Sundays or just at night when we say our prayers. Serving God is an all-the-time thing because love is also an all-the-time thing. Every time you decide not to be selfish, you are choosing to love—and you are serving God!

• •

Lord God, please show me all
sorts of ways to serve You.

Prejudice

Many people in that town of Samaria believed in Jesus because of what the woman said about Him.
JOHN 4:39

Prejudice means we think someone is not as good as we are because of the way that person looks or acts or talks. It's a big problem today—and it was also a big problem when Jesus was on earth. When Jesus was on earth, His people—the Jews—did not get along with a group of people called the Samaritans. The Jews hated the Samaritans and thought they were better than them. But Jesus knew better. He wasn't prejudiced. Jesus knew God loves all of us. And He wants us to love *all* people the same way He loves us.

• •

Lord God, help me to love others without prejudice, the same way You love everyone.

Shiny and Beautiful

"I will set your stones in beautiful colors. You will stand upon blue stones of much worth."
ISAIAH **54:11**

Do you ever feel like no one really sees you? This verse from the book of Isaiah tells you that you are precious in God's eyes. It tells you that God is working inside you to make you even more beautiful. He is building your life into something sparkling and new. Close your eyes and imagine it for a moment. Can you see yourself standing on a bright blue stone that glows with God's love? Can you see yourself shining with God's love? That's the way God sees you!

. . . .

Thank You, Father God, that Your love is making me shiny and beautiful.

Named by God

"I will give each of them a white stone also. A new name will be written on it. No one will know the name except the one who receives it!"
REVELATION 2:17

Names are important. They help us know who we are. In this verse, when Jesus says He will give you a new name, He means He sees who you really are, in a way no one else can see, not even your parents or your closest friends. He knows you even better than you know yourself! The name He gives you stands for everything God wants you to be—and if you let Him, Jesus will help you grow into that "you," the very best you!

• •

Thank You, Jesus, that You have a special name for me.

The Helper

*"The Helper is the Holy Spirit. . . .
He will teach you everything and help
you remember everything I have told you."*
JOHN **14:26**

The Holy Spirit is part of God, just like Jesus is part of God. God is so big that you'll never understand everything about Him—but the Holy Spirit is the way God can live inside you. The Spirit is also the way Jesus can be with you always, even though you can't see Him or touch Him. The Holy Spirit lives inside you, teaching you about God. He will help you remember the things you've learned about God in the Bible. He will be with you all the time. And if you make more room for the Holy Spirit inside you, He'll help you more and more.

• •

Holy Spirit, teach me how to listen to You.

God's Paintbrush

We know that God makes all things work together for the good of those who love Him.
ROMANS 8:28

Some things are just so big and so bad that they seem bigger than God. But the same God who made the world the stars and the sun and our planet with all its animals and plants and people—this *same* God is also busy in your life. Your life is like a beautiful picture that God is painting. You might make a big mess right in the middle of it. But there's good news! God's love is like an amazing paintbrush that turns even ugly things into beautiful things.

. . . .

Thank You, Lord God, that my life is like a beautiful picture You are painting for all the world to see.

Off Course

*We may be dead to sin and alive
to all that is right and good.*
1 PETER 2:24

When a snake grows, its skin doesn't grow with it—so every now and then, the snake has to completely shed its old dead skin so it can grow bigger. The sin in our lives is like that old snakeskin. We need to shed our sins—the things that make God unhappy—completely. Then we can grow into the loving people God wants us to be. God wants you to get rid of the old, selfish part of you so that you can grow strong and beautiful.

. . . .

*Father God, I want to be the brand-new me
who is learning more about You every day.*

The Good Shepherd

*The Lord is my Shepherd. I will
have everything I need.*
PSALM 23:1

When David was still a boy, he took care of sheep. When he wrote this verse, comparing God to a shepherd, he knew that sheep need shepherds to take care of them. Shepherds show sheep where to go. Shepherds keep their sheep safe from wild animals, and they make sure their sheep have enough to eat and drink. Shepherds look for their sheep when they're lost, and they rescue their sheep when they're in trouble. And those are all things God will do for you! He'll take care of you and watch over you—always!

· ·

*Thank You, Lord God, that You take care of me
the way a good shepherd takes care of sheep.*

An Acorn

*"Unless a seed falls into the ground
and dies, it will only be a seed."*
JOHN 12:24

Think about an acorn (which is a kind of seed). If you bury an acorn and let it break into pieces under the dirt, one day you might see a little green leaf pushing up through the soil. If you wait long enough, the acorn will grow into a tall, beautiful tree.

In this Bible verse, Jesus uses a seed to help you understand how to grow. A part of you will have to break, the same way the acorn did. The part of you that wants to do whatever you want—the selfish part—is the part that needs to break. Once that happens, the *real* you inside will grow bigger and more wonderful than you could ever imagine.

* *

Jesus, I want to grow more and more like You.

Tell God Everything

Pour out your heart before Him.
God is a safe place for us.
PSALM 62:8

God loves for you to tell Him everything you think and feel. When you're confused, He wants to listen and help you understand. When you're happy, He wants to smile with you. When you're sad, He wants to wrap His love around you and help you feel better. When you're mad, He listens and helps you cool down. You can even tell Him if you're mad at *Him*. He wants to hear it all! You can tell Him anything, and He'll never get upset with you. You are completely safe with Him. And He loves to hear your voice!

• •

Thank You, Father God, that You want
to hear all my thoughts and feelings.

35

You Make God Sing

"The Lord your God. . .will have joy
over you with loud singing."
ZEPHANIAH 3:17

You make God happy! Think about that. The same God who made the earth, the sun, moon, and stars, the oceans and mountains—He is the same God who loves you. He loves to see you and hear you. When you talk to God, when you're kind to other people, when you do things to make the world more beautiful, God smiles. In fact, you make Him so happy that He bursts out in song! He sings a song that belongs only to you.

· ·

Lord God, I want to make You smile and
sing. Show me how to make You happy.

God's Children

See what great love the Father has for us that He would call us His children.
1 JOHN 3:1

John, the man who wrote this verse, got to spend time with Jesus. He and Jesus had long face-to-face talks. Jesus taught John that God loves you and me the same way He loves His Son, Jesus. You are God's son or daughter, just like Jesus is God's Son. God takes care of you and watches over you, the way good parents love and watch over their children. God doesn't want you to be scared of Him. He doesn't want you to feel like He's too far away to care about what's going on in your life. He wants you to know you're His very own child, and He loves you!

* *

Father God, thank You that I'm Your child.

Wait for God

Wait for the Lord. Be strong.
PSALM 27:14

Sometimes it seems like God is taking *forever* to do something. And we get tired of waiting. The Bible tells us that sometimes waiting is just a part of God's plan for us. Waiting for God without complaining is a way to say to God, "Do whatever You want with me—and do it *whenever* You want." Waiting for God means you stop saying, "I want it—and I want it *now*!" You know that God always does things in the best way. And so, while you wait, you let God teach you new things. And then, when at last the right time comes, you're ready for whatever God wants to do in your life!

• •

Lord God, please help me to wait for You.

Starting Over

O Lord, be kind to us. We have waited for You. Be our strength every morning. Save us in the time of trouble.
ISAIAH **33:2**

Every day is a brand-new chance to follow God. It doesn't matter if you messed up today—because tomorrow, God will let you begin again. If you were selfish today or mean to someone, tonight is your chance to tell God you're sorry. You can ask Him to help you do better tomorrow. If you hurt someone's feelings or disappointed someone today, you can ask God tonight what you can do tomorrow to make things better. So tomorrow, when you first wake up, ask God to help you with the new day He's given you.

. . . .

Thank You, Lord God, that You always let me start over.

Whatever You Need

"The Lord will give us what we need."
GENESIS 22:14

God is taking care of you. He is making sure you have what you need to grow and be healthy and happy. But sometimes you may feel like this isn't true. *If God is taking care of me,* you may think, *why do bad things happen sometimes? Why don't I have all the toys I want? Why isn't everyone nice to me all the time?* But God is like any good parent—He doesn't always give you what you think you want. God knows what you *really* need. And if He doesn't answer your prayers the way you want, it's because He loves you so much and knows what is truly best for you.

. . . .

*Father God, thank You that You love
me so much. Help me to understand
when You don't answer my prayers the
way I think You should. I trust You.*

Smile!

This is the day that the Lord has made.
Let us be full of joy and be glad in it.
PSALM **118:24**

Jesus doesn't want His followers to go around with sad faces. He wants them to smile and laugh and play. In fact, He wants them to be more like children! The Bible is stuffed full of happy words—words like *glad*, *joy*, *dance*, *sing*. Nowhere does the Bible say, "Be sad. Frown. Worry." God wants to make you happy! And then He wants you to share your happiness with all the people around you. Your smiles can make others smile. Your kindness can bring people joy. Each day is a chance for you to serve God by making people happy.

* *

Lord God, tomorrow when I wake up,
I want to start out with a smile.

What We Need Today

"Give us the bread we need today."
MATTHEW 6:11

When Jesus said these words about bread, He wasn't talking only about food. He was talking about all the things you need to grow—things like love and attention from the grown-ups in your life, friendships with people your age, new things to learn, chances to play and have fun, and times when you get to know God better. God doesn't give you everything you need all at once. Sometimes you might have to wait to get something. But one day at a time, He will give you everything you need to grow and be the person He wants you to be.

• •

Thank You, Father, that You give
me what I need every day.

God Is Love

God is love.
1 JOHN 4:8

John, the man who wrote this verse, was best friends with Jesus. When Jesus was on earth, He and John spent a lot of time together. They talked about all sorts of things, the way all friends do. All that time with Jesus gave John a special understanding of God. John knew that when it comes right down to it, God is very simple—He is love. This means that God is never selfish. He doesn't hold back but instead gives everything away. He gives and gives and gives. And when you act the same way—when you love people enough not to be selfish—then God is living right inside you!

* *

*Lord, I know what love is—and
that means I know You!*

Where Do You Live?

Lord, You have been the place of comfort for all people of all time.
PSALM 90:1

Do you know what a "place of comfort" is? It's a place where you feel safe, a place where you feel loved. That place might be your home, where you live with your family. It's where you keep the things that are most important to you. In this verse, David is saying that God is your home. God is like a place where you go to be safe, a place where you are loved so very much. You don't just visit God. You don't come and go. God is your forever home, no matter what happens.

• •

Thank You, Lord God, that You will always be my home.

I Want It!

"Watch yourselves! Keep from wanting all kinds of things you should not have."
LUKE **12:15**

Do you ever see an advertisement for a toy or game and think, *I want it*? Or when you go shopping with a grown-up, do you see all the bright-colored things on the shelves and think, *I want those*? You might feel like you'll never be happy if you can't get the things you want. It's easy to want, want, want. In this Bible verse, Jesus says, "Be careful about all that wanting!" He knows that when you want something too much, you end up thinking only about yourself. You don't really care about other people. You forget about God. Wanting can be a big problem!

Father God, help me to be happy with the things You have already given me.

Look Up!

*I will lay my prayers before
You and will look up.*
PSALM 5:3

When you talk to God, do you ever stop to listen to see if
He has something He wants to say to you? God loves when
you tell Him everything. But He also likes you to take a few
minutes to listen to Him. This means you stop talking and
look up. You stop thinking about yourself and all the things
going on in your life. You pay attention to God instead. You
probably won't hear an actual voice talking to you. You may
not hear anything at all. But just being quiet, waiting, and
listening for God is good for you. And it lets God know how
much you love Him.

*Dear Lord, thank You for listening to me
and knowing exactly what I need. Help me
to hear the things You want me to know.*

Fruit

The fruit that comes from having the Holy Spirit in our lives is: love, joy, peace, not giving up, being kind, being good, having faith.
GALATIANS 5:22

When an apple tree is healthy, it makes fruit. The same is true when the Holy Spirit lives inside you. He makes "fruit" in your life. This fruit isn't apples or oranges or cherries. It's love, joy, peace, not giving up, being kind, being good, having faith. First, you make room for the Holy Spirit by getting your selfishness out of the way—and then He'll do His job. The more you make room for the Holy Spirit to live in you, the more good things will grow out of your life.

• •

Holy Spirit, help me to make room for You so that You can fill my life with love, kindness, and joy.

Always the Same

*Jesus Christ is the same yesterday
and today and forever.*
HEBREWS **13:8**

Do you like when things change? Or do changes make you
feel scared or unhappy? School is a place where each year
brings changes. When one school year ends and another
begins, you will probably have a new teacher and a new
classroom. You will learn and do new things. You might
make new friends. The new classroom might seem strange
and not as nice as your old one. That can be a sad change.
Change is like that. It brings good things into your life—and
it takes other things away. Change is just a part of life that
never goes away. So it's good to know that one thing never
changes: the Lord God!

• •

Thank You, Father God, that You never change.

The Gift of Friendship

A friend loves at all times.
PROVERBS 17:17

Everybody needs friends. Your friends help you have more fun when you play. They listen when you tell them things. Friends are special gifts from God, and friendship is one way you can learn more about how to follow God. Friendship gives you chances to practice sharing your toys. It gives you chances to take turns. Friendship also gives you lots of chances to say you're sorry. Even though friends get mad and fight, they always make up. They teach each other how to get along with other people. Sharing, taking turns, and saying you're sorry are important lessons you'll need your whole life, even when you're a grown-up.

· ·

Jesus, thank You for being the best friend I'll ever have.

Good News

Faith comes to us by hearing the Good News.
ROMANS 10:17

Faith is one of those words that can be hard to understand. This Bible verse tells us that faith is something that comes to you the more you listen to the good news. The good news is that God loves you so much that He sent Jesus to show you His love. When you follow Jesus, you get to live forever with Him, even after you die. So how can you listen to this good news more? You can hear it by paying attention at church and Sunday school. You can hear it by reading the Bible. And you can hear it by listening to the Holy Spirit talking right to you inside your heart.

• •

Thank You, Jesus, for bringing the wonderful news that God loves me.

Stop Being Angry!

Stop being angry. Turn away from fighting.
PSALM 37:8

We all get angry sometimes. Being mad isn't a sin. It doesn't mean we're bad. But the Bible says we shouldn't *stay* mad. When we're angry, we can lose track of what God wants us to do. We can say mean things and hurt people's feelings. That's why the Bible says that when we get mad, we should let go of our angry feelings, not hold on to them. Instead of stomping around and shouting—or sitting alone and thinking mad thoughts—we can do something else that gets our minds off our angry feelings. Things like drawing a picture, reading a book, or playing outside can help us stop feeling so mad.

• •

Father God, when I get mad, remind me
to talk to You about my feelings.

In the Dark

Who. . .obeys the voice of His Servant,
yet walks in darkness and has no
light? Let him trust in the name of the
Lord and have faith in his God.
ISAIAH **50:10**

The Bible promises you that you don't need to be afraid of the dark. God is there, and He will take care of you. But sometimes when the Bible talks about darkness, it's not talking about nighttime or a room with no lights on. Instead, it's talking about a feeling we get that everything is bad and sad. We might think that feeling is because we did something wrong. But those scary times aren't punishments from God. We didn't do anything wrong. No matter how bad, sad, or scary life may seem, God is with us.

• •

Thank You, Lord, that even when I
can't see, You see everything.

Love's Rainbow

Love does not give up. Love is kind. Love is not jealous. Love does not put itself up as being important. Love has no pride. Love does not do the wrong thing. Love never thinks of itself. Love does not get angry. Love does not remember the suffering that comes from being hurt by someone. . . . Love takes everything that comes without giving up.
1 CORINTHIANS 13:4–5, 7

Love is a little like a rainbow. It has a lot of "colors." These verses make a list of all the colors in love's rainbow:

- Not giving up
- Being kind
- Not being jealous of other people
- Not thinking you're more important or better than others
- Not doing wrong things
- Not being selfish
- Forgiving people who have hurt you

Dear Father God, may my life shine like a rainbow with Your love.

When You're Scared

"Do not be afraid or troubled.
Be strong and have strength of heart."
JOSHUA 10:25

We all feel scared and sad sometimes. We just can't help it. Even Jesus felt scared and sad when He was on earth. But when we have those sad, scared feelings, we need to hold on extra tight to God. We need to think about Him and talk to Him and talk *about* Him even more than usual. Those sad, bad feelings are just feelings. They will only last awhile, and then they'll go away. But God's love lasts forever!

. . . .

Help me, Lord, to think about You the next
time I'm sad or scared. Help me to remember
that bad feelings always go away. Thank
You that Your love never goes away!

The New You

The old life is gone. New life has begun.
2 CORINTHIANS 5:17

A man named Paul wrote these words in a letter to his friends. Paul wanted his friends to understand that God gives us a brand-new way to live. We don't have to be selfish anymore—and we don't have to feel guilty about the selfish things we used to do. We are living a new life now. We are living God's life because the Holy Spirit is inside us, helping us to grow and learn. Our new lives are happier and more exciting than our old lives ever were. And our new lives will never end!

• •

Father God, tomorrow when I wake up, remind me that every day is part of my new life with You.

Free!

You are free from the power of sin.
You have become a servant for God.
ROMANS 6:22

A bad habit is something you keep doing that hurts you or other people. You don't mean to keep doing it. You just do it without even thinking about it. Picking at mosquito bites until they bleed could be a bad habit. Telling lies might be a bad habit too. Selfishness is a habit that pretty much all people have, but that doesn't make it okay.

Breaking the habit of selfishness isn't easy. But God wants to break all your selfish habits. He wants you to be free to love Him and other people the same way He loves you.

• •

Jesus, help me to break my selfish, bad habits
so I can be free to love the way You do.

Learning Love

We love Him because He loved us first.
1 JOHN 4:19

Babies learn to love by being loved. Little kids like to copy what older people do, so when they copy the people who love them, they learn how to show their love to others. The same thing is true with God. The more time you spend with God, the more You'll feel His love. The more you feel His love, the more You'll love Him. The more You love Him, the more He will help you love other people. It's like when you throw a stone in the water—it makes circles that get bigger and bigger and bigger. And it all starts with God's love.

· ·

Teach me to love, Lord God.

Doubt

The Lord said to him, "Who has made man's mouth? . . . I will be with your mouth. I will teach you what to say."
EXODUS 4:11–12

In this Bible story from the book of Exodus, God asked Moses to do something important—but Moses said, "Sorry, God. I'm too shy. I don't like to talk in front of people. I'd like to do what You ask, but I just can't." Have you ever felt like that? Have you ever said to yourself, *I'd like to show people I love them—but I'm too shy, and I don't know what to say*? If so, the God who made the world is big enough to help you, just like He helped Moses. God will teach you what to say and do.

• •

*Lord God, when I doubt myself,
help me not to doubt You.*

God Is All Around

*"It is in Him that we live and
move and keep on living."*
ACTS 17:28

Think about a fish in the water. The water is all around that
fish. Everywhere the fish goes, the water is always there.
The fish gets its food from that water. It lives its whole life in
the water. If you took the fish out of the water, it would die.
God is a little like water—and you are a little like a fish! God
is all around us. You will live your whole life surrounded by
God. Without God to sustain you, you would die. But God
never goes away. He is always there. So long as you live in
God, you will be safe forever.

• •

*Father God, thank You that You are
all around me all the time.*

Forgotten

"I will not forget you."
ISAIAH **49:15**

Have you ever waited and waited for a grown-up to do something—and then found out that they forgot? Maybe someone even forgot to pick you up on time after school. They didn't mean to forget you. They just got busy, and now they're sorry. Hopefully, you can forgive the person who made you wait, but it's still a sad, scary feeling when someone forgets you. But God never, ever forgets you. Even when you can't tell He's with you, He's right there, all around you. He never gets too busy, and He never forgets. He is always with you.

• •

Lord God, thank You that You never forget me.

Arguments

There was fighting all around us.
Our hearts were afraid. But God gives
comfort to those whose hearts are heavy.
2 CORINTHIANS 7:5–6

All human beings, big and little, have arguments sometimes. They're just a part of life. When you get in an argument, the best way to end it is to say you're sorry and make up. But what do you do when grown-ups argue? You can't *make* them say they're sorry. But you might tell them how you feel when they fight. You can ask them to try to find a way to make up. And if they won't listen to you, you can talk to God about it. He understands how you feel, and He will help.

• •

Father God, when I get in an argument, help me
to say I'm sorry before too much time goes by.

Bad News

*He will not be afraid of bad news. His heart
is strong because he trusts in the Lord.*
PSALM 112:7

No one likes to hear bad news. Bad news comes in all kinds
of shapes. It takes you by surprise. It makes you feel sad and
scared. Some people get so worried about bad news that
they can't ever be happy because they're always thinking
something bad will happen. Bad things do happen sometimes.
That's just the way life is. But you don't have to worry about
those things happening ahead of time. If they happen, God
will be there with you. You can trust Him.

• •

*I'm glad, Lord, that I don't have to worry
about bad news because I have You.*

No Fear

God is our safe place and our strength.
He is always our help when we are in trouble.
PSALM **46:1**

Fear can keep us from doing something dangerous. Being scared can help keep us safe. It can tell us when we should run away. But sometimes we get scared when nothing really dangerous is happening. We might be scared of a friendly dog. We might be afraid of bugs that won't actually hurt us. We might get scared in certain places or with certain people who are completely harmless. God doesn't want you to have those kinds of fears. He wants you to know that He is always with you. You can tell Him about anything that seems scary in your life, and He will help you.

. . . .

Thank You, Father, that You
are taking care of me.

Best Friends with God

*If sinners try to lead you into
sin, do not go with them.*
PROVERBS 1:10

The book of Proverbs was written by a very wise man. He knew how easy it is to go along with what our friends do, even when we know it's wrong. It can be really hard to say no to a friend. You want to make your friends happy. You want them to like you. Sometimes you might feel mixed up inside. You might know that something isn't right, but your friends make you wonder if you're wrong. That's why you need to be best friends with God. You need to talk to Him and listen to Him. He will help you know what the right thing to do is—and He will help you do it.

. . . .

I want to be best friends with You, Lord God.

Shout!

"Cry with a loud voice. Do not hold back. Raise your voice like a horn."
Isaiah **58:1**

There's a story in the Bible about a city called Jericho. God wanted His people to capture the city but not to hurt anyone. So God told His people to march around the city walls once a day for six days while the priests blew trumpets. On the seventh day, God told His people to march around the city seven times and then to give a loud shout. When they did, the walls fell down! God probably doesn't want you to knock down any walls. But He does want you to spread His love to everyone. You and your friends can work together to make that happen.

* *

Lord God, when I feel shy, help my friends to give me courage. And when they feel shy, remind me to help them.

Always Thinking of You

Your thoughts are of great worth to me, O God.
PSALM 139:17

Have you ever wondered what God thinks about? *You* are always on His mind. He sees everything you do. He knows your every thought. He listens to everything you say. He cries when you cry, and He laughs when you laugh. He understands you better than any other person can. He knows when you're strong and good, and He knows when you feel small and weak. He's thinking about you every minute of every day and every night. And He is always with you, waiting for you to think about Him—to call on Him for help, for love, for anything you need.

. . . .

Father God, thank You that You are
always thinking about me.

Weakness

The Holy Spirit helps us where we are weak.
ROMANS 8:26

When your body is weak, it can't do all the things you want to do. Sometimes being sick can make you so weak you can't run around and play the way you usually do. You might be weak just because you're still small. You can also be weak on the inside, in your heart and your mind. When that happens, you might not be able to be as loving as you know God wants you to be. But don't worry! God doesn't ever get mad at you for being weak. Instead, He sends the Holy Spirit to help you. The weaker you are, the more you need God—and the more you need God, the more He will help you.

• •

When I'm weak, Lord, I'm glad Your Holy Spirit is right there waiting to help me.

God Is Enough

*My soul is quiet and waits for God
alone. My hope comes from Him.*
PSALM 62:5

No matter how much people really, truly love you, they will hurt your feelings sooner or later. But God never will. That's what our good friend David was saying when he wrote this verse. David knew that God is the only one who will never, ever let us down. David didn't expect people to give what only God can give. David was counting on God, not other people. David knew that even when other people got mad at him or hurt him, God was everything he needed. God's love was all he needed to be happy.

. . . .

*Thank You, Father, that I can
always count on You.*

Healing

"I will heal them."
JEREMIAH **33:6**

The Bible has many messages that it says over and over, and this is one of them—God heals us. This means that when you're sick, you can ask God to help you get better. But God also wants to heal anything that hurts inside your heart and mind. He wants to make your thoughts and feelings healthy and good. Sometimes God might even let your body get sick so you have more time to think about Him. It's not that He ever wants you to hurt or feel bad, but He can use everything—even being sick—to help you become the person He wants you to be. The healing He wants to give you will last forever.

* *

Heal me, Lord God, inside and out.

Lies

"Do not follow many people in doing wrong."
EXODUS 23:2

Have you ever heard one of your friends tell a story you knew wasn't true? Maybe the story was about another kid. Maybe it was a mean story, but it was also really funny, and you couldn't help laughing when you heard it. And then maybe you told someone else that story and made them laugh. And they told someone else. . . . The story might have hurt people's feelings. It might have gotten someone in trouble. It made people believe something that wasn't true. That's why the Bible tells you to be careful about what you say. God doesn't want you to go along with lies—not ever.

• •

*Help me, Father, to be strong enough
to speak up for what is true.*

70

Riches

"Wherever your riches are,
your heart will be there also."
MATTHEW 6:21

What are your riches? Maybe you think that riches are money, but that's not always true. In the Bible, riches are anything you care about a lot. They're your treasure! Your treasure might be your toys, your pets, your friends, your family, your clothes, or your computer games. These aren't bad things. But Jesus wants you to be careful about what you care about most. He wants you to remember that love is always the most important thing in life. And He wants to be your treasure, the thing you care about more than anything else.

I want You to be my treasure, Jesus. You're
more important to me than anything else.

God Is Great

The Lord is great. . .too great
for anyone to understand.
PSALM **145:3**

No one knows all there is to know about God. There is always more to learn. No matter how long you live or how much you learn, you will always be learning new things about God. And if you ever stop learning—if you ever think you've learned everything about God—then you're in trouble! People who think they know everything stop learning. They stop being open to what God wants to teach them. God wants you to spend every day of the rest of your life getting to know Him better and better. You'll never run out of things to learn.

• •

Lord God, I want to learn whatever You
want to teach me about Yourself.

Good Things

"I will bring good to you."
Genesis 12:2

Sometimes you might think God is bringing something really bad to you—and then later you realize it was something good all along. Maybe your mom or dad got a new job and your family had to move to a new town. That seemed like a really bad thing when it happened. But then you made new friends at your new school. In fact, you made friends with someone who became the best friend you ever had. You never know what will happen. But you can count on this—God is always, always bringing good to you.

· ·

Thank You, Father God, that even when I feel sad about something that happens, You are still bringing good things into my life.

God's Plan

*We are His work. He has made us to belong
to Christ Jesus so we can work for Him.
He planned that we should do this.*
EPHESIANS 2:10

Did you know that God has special jobs He wants you to do for Him? His plans for you start right now when you're a kid. How can you know God's plans for your life? First, you should spend time talking to Him every day. Read the Bible. Listen when people who know God talk about Him. The more you get to know God, the more you will understand what jobs He has given you to do. Whatever His plans for you are, you can count on this—God's plans will make you happy, and they'll make the people around you happy too.

· ·

Lord God, what is Your plan for me?

God's Goodness

"Give thanks to the Lord, for He is good."
1 CHRONICLES 16:34

"What does it mean to be good?" a Sunday school teacher asked her class.

"It means you don't get in trouble," said one boy.

"What sort of things get you in trouble?" the teacher asked.

"Stealing," the children said. "Telling lies. Saying mean things."

"So," the teacher said, "being good means being kind to others and doing our best not to hurt them in any way. Now here's another question—is God good?"

The children nodded their heads.

"Well, what does that mean?" Everyone was quiet, so the teacher said, "When we say God is good, we're saying He is kind. Everything He does—even the things we don't understand or don't like—all of it is done because He loves us."

"So being good is like loving," said one of the children.

The teacher smiled. "Exactly!"

. . . .

Father God, I'm so glad You are good.

Worry

Perfect love puts fear out of our hearts.
1 John 4:18

Do you ever worry? Worry is a way of being scared—but it's not the sort of scared you might feel when a big dog growls at you or when you dive off a diving board into a pool. Worry is being afraid of something that *might* happen. And guess what? Worry tells lies. A lot of the time, the things we worry about never happen. And even if they do happen, God is right there with us, helping us. So instead of worrying about what's going to happen, try praying about it! God loves you, and He has everything under control.

• •

Lord God, the next time I start to worry, help me to remember how much You love me.

A Broken Heart

*The Lord is near to those who
have a broken heart.*
PSALM **34:18**

When you are very sad, it can feel like your heart breaks. This isn't the kind of little sadness that goes away quickly. It's a big sadness that stays and stays. It's there when you wake up in the morning, and it's still there when you fall asleep at night. It just doesn't go away. It's a great big hurting feeling inside your chest. The good thing, though, is that God stays especially near to people when their hearts are hurting. During those sad, sad times, you can learn more about God. His love wraps around your heart—and one day, He will take the pain away. You can trust Him to do that.

. . . .

Thank You, Father, that You heal broken hearts.

Turning Around

"Be sorry for your sins. . . . Turn your faces away from all your sinful ways."
EZEKIEL **14:6**

The Bible says that it's not enough to feel sorry for the way we've been living. We also have to turn away from all those sins. Imagine walking down a path and then realizing the path was leading you away from God. Just feeling sad that you were going in the wrong direction wouldn't do you any good. You'd have to turn around and start walking in a different direction. You'd have to get on the path that leads you to God.

- -

Show me, Lord, whenever I get on the wrong path. I want to always walk toward You.

78

God's Favor

"Now is the right time! See!
Now is the day to be saved."
2 CORINTHIANS 6:2

Do you ever wish that every other day was Christmas—and the days in between were your birthday? It's hard to wait each year for Christmas and birthdays to come around again. But every year you just have to wait for the weeks and months to go by. You don't ever have to wait for God to show you His love, though. Even on boring days when nothing much seems to happen, even on sad days or scary days, God is right there. It's always the right time to pay attention to what God is doing in your life!

• •

Thank You, Father God, that You are always
ready to love me. I never have to wait.

My Banner

The Lord is My Banner.
EXODUS 17:15

In the Bible, Moses gave God a special name. He called God "My Banner." That seems like a funny name, doesn't it? Moses was talking about the flag that an army carried when it marched into battle. When the soldiers saw the banner blowing in the wind, they felt happier. They knew that if they got lost or got into trouble, all they had to do was look until they saw that flag. It would tell them where to go.

God is like that. God's love is right there with you whenever you face something hard. If you feel lost or sad or scared, look until you see His love. He will show you the way.

• •

Thank You, Lord, that You are a banner of love, showing me the way to go.

Worry Stoppers

"Do not worry. . . . Your Father in heaven knows you need all these things."
MATTHEW 6:31–32

When you have a problem that makes you feel scared or worried, here are some things you can do that will help you feel happier.

- Think about God. Talk to Him. Tell Him your troubles.
- Think about other people in your life. And then pray for them.
- Try thinking about your problem in a new way. Pretend you are someone else, and imagine how they would think about this problem.
- Go out of your way to be nice to someone else. Notice who needs help, and do what you can to help them.

. . . .

Thank You, Father, that You always love me and You always give me what I need.

Hope from God

Our hope comes from God.
ROMANS 15:13

We all say things like "I hope the sun shines tomorrow." Or "I hope you can come to my house next week." But when the Bible talks about hope, it's not talking about wishing or wanting. The Bible's hope is the way God wants us to think about the future. Hope is how God wants us to face tomorrow and next week and next year. Nothing will ever happen—not today, not tomorrow, not next year or ten years from now or a hundred years from now—that will put an end to God's love. That's what hope really means—it means counting on God's love.

* *

God of hope, thank You that I can count on Your love tomorrow—and for the rest of my life.

Secrets

"The Lord looks at the heart."
1 SAMUEL 16:7

God sees all your secrets. You can't hide anything from Him. And He loves you so much that He hates to see you carrying something ugly around with you. He knows that ugly secret will make you sad. As time goes by, it will make you a little sick inside your heart. It will come between you and the love God wants to give you. So whenever you have a secret like that, the best thing to do is to give it to God. He will show you what you should do next—and whatever it is, He'll be right there with you.

. . . .

Lord God, I don't want to keep secrets from You.

What God Wants Done

*"What You want done, may it be
done on earth as it is in heaven."*
MATTHEW 6:10

This verse is part of the prayer that Jesus taught His friends
to pray. Some people call it the "Lord's Prayer." This prayer
shows us how Jesus wants us to talk to God. Jesus' prayer
is simple. It just says, "Father God, do whatever You want,
the same way here on earth, in my life, as You're doing in
heaven." How does God do things in heaven? Well, we can't
really know—but we do know that everything God does is
done in love. And we know that in heaven, no sin or selfishness gets in the way of God's love.

• •

*Dear Lord, I want Your love to run my life.
I want to help You build a world that's as
beautiful and full of love as heaven is.*

Absolutely Sure

*"I know that the One Who. . .made
me free from sin lives, and that He will
stand upon the earth in the end. . . .
With my own eyes I will see Him."*
JOB 19:25, 27

Job was a man in the Bible who had all kinds of terrible things happen to him. The people he loved died. He got sick. Just about everything that could go wrong for Job went wrong! But Job said, "I know that God is still alive. No matter how awful things look right now, I'm sure that God is still in charge. And I know that one day I'm going to see God face-to-face." When bad things happen, sometimes it seems like God doesn't love us after all. But that is never true. God is alive! God loves us! We can count on that.

• •

Father God, help me to be sure that You love me.

Look inside Your Heart

The Lord of All says, "Think about your ways!"
HAGGAI 1:7

Do you ever just take for granted that you are a good kid?
Your parents love you, your friends like you, and your teach-
ers give you decent grades. So that means you're a good
kid, right? Well, yes, you *are* a good kid—but not because
of those things. You are good because God loves you. But
sometimes He wants you to look inside yourself. Are you
really as good as everyone thinks? God wants you to be
honest with yourself. He doesn't want anything inside you
to come between you and His love.

• •

*Dear Lord, help me to see inside my own heart.
Help me to grow more and more like Jesus.*

What's Fair

*He loves what is right and
good and what is fair.*
PSALM 33:5

You probably have a pretty good idea about what's fair and
what's not. When someone shoves to the front of the line,
that's not fair. When someone cheats during a game, that's
not fair either.

God wants things to be fair. The Bible says so over and
over. The Bible also says it's our job to help make things fair.
God asks us to share what we have with those who have less
than us (Proverbs 22:16). He asks us to be kind to strangers
who are far from home (Exodus 22:21). He tells us to do
"what is right and good and what is fair."

. . . .

*Help me to copy You, Jesus. I want to
make the world a fairer place.*

Goodness Everywhere

Many words will come from their
mouths about how good You are.
PSALM 145:7

The world is full of God's goodness. Look around, and you'll
see it everywhere. Look up at the sky. Look at the trees and
grass and plants. Look at sunrises and sunsets. Listen to
birds singing and the wind rustling through the trees. Taste
your favorite food. Drink a big glass of water when you're
thirsty. Feel the softness of the blanket on your skin as you
lie in bed. Breathe in the smell of cookies baking. See the
love in your family's eyes. All these things show you the
goodness of God. It's everywhere you turn!

• •

Lord God, thank You for all the
good things in my life.

Simply Silly

A glad heart is good medicine.
PROVERBS 17:22

Being sad all the time can make you feel tired. It can even make your head ache or make you sick. Being scared can make your stomach ache. But being happy makes your body feel better. Smiling and laughing can take away the yucky feelings. Being silly and giggling is good for you! Of course some times are better for silliness than others. When your teacher is in the middle of a lesson or your pastor is preaching a sermon, your job is to listen, not giggle! But every day should have time for silliness. God loves to hear you laugh!

Father God, thank You that You are right there with me when I'm happy.

Everything Is Possible!

"God can do anything."
MARK 10:27

A long, long time ago, God told a man named Abraham to go outdoors and look up at the night sky. "See those stars, Abraham?" God asked. "That's how many children and grandchildren and great-grandchildren and great-great-too-many-times-to-count-great-grandchildren you're going to have." Abraham was sure this was impossible. He and his wife were old, and they didn't have any children. And yet, Abraham believed God's promise—and God did the impossible.

God still does impossible things. So keep your eyes open. Believe in God the way Abraham did. God can do anything.

. . . .

Thank You, Lord, that Your love is so strong it can do things that seem impossible.

God's Long Arm

*"The Lord your God brought you out of
there by a powerful hand and a long arm."*
DEUTERONOMY 5:15

Sometimes God can seem very far away. He might seem so far away that it's hard for you to believe He can help you with your life. But the Bible says God has a long arm. The Bible is not talking about God's actual arm, like yours. It's saying that no matter how far away God may seem, His love can always reach you. And God doesn't just have a long arm. He also has a strong hand. No problem you could ever have would be too big for God to handle. His love is strong!

• •

*Father God, thank You for reaching out
to me no matter how far away I feel.*

Get Out of God's Way

Give all your cares to the Lord and
He will give you strength.
PSALM 55:22

If you want God to help you with your problems, first you have to get out of His way. You do that by saying to God, "I don't know how to handle this problem. I've tried to figure it out and I can't. But I know You can handle everything, so I'm going to get out of Your way and let You work. I'm giving this problem to You. It's all Yours now. Please show me what You want me to do. Make me strong enough to do what You want." When you pray like that, you give Him space to work.

• •

Lord God, show me if I'm getting in Your
way by trying to do things all by myself.

Too Tired

*They who wait upon the Lord will
get new strength. They will rise
up with wings like eagles.*
ISAIAH 40:31

Do you ever feel tired of trying to be good? No matter how
hard you try, sooner or later you mess up. Even when you're
trying *really* hard to be good, the grown-ups in your life
don't seem to notice. Sometimes you might want to just
give up and be bad.

God understands that feeling. But as with everything else
in your life, He wants you to bring that feeling to Him. When
you talk to Him about how you feel, He'll help you keep going
even though you're tired.

- -

*When I'm tired of being good, Lord,
give me what I need to keep going.*

Life and Love That Last Forever

"For God so loved the world that He gave His only Son. Whoever puts his trust in God's Son will not be lost but will have life that lasts forever."
JOHN 3:16

A lot of people know this verse by heart. But do you know what it *really* means? It's the good news, the message Jesus came to tell us. If we break it down into pieces, it looks like this:

- God loves you.
- God gives you His Son.
- When you trust Jesus—when you give your life to Him—He'll always be with you. He won't let you get lost or separated from Him.
- Because of Jesus, your life will last forever, even after you die.

Isn't that amazing?

• •

Thank You, Jesus, that Your love takes care of me and gives me life.

While You're Sleeping

He Who watches over you will not sleep.
PSALM **121:3**

People need to go to sleep every night—but God doesn't. While you're sleeping tonight, He'll be watching over you. He'll stay up all night, taking care of you as you sleep. He'll even be with you in your dreams, and if you have a nightmare, He'll be right there to comfort you. So don't worry about anything as you go to sleep tonight. God is taking care of everything. You can trust Him.

- -

Father God, I'm so glad You don't need to sleep. Thank You that You will be watching me and loving me as I sleep tonight.

Even Better!

God is able to do much more than we ask
or think through His power working in us.
EPHESIANS 3:20

Close your eyes and imagine something you'd like God to do. It doesn't matter what it is. God is strong enough to do something even better than what you are imagining. So now imagine that there's *more* of whatever you're thinking about. Picture it bigger. God can still do more! This doesn't mean God really will do what you're imagining. God isn't like a magic genie who grants you wishes. And what you are imagining might not actually be good for you, and God never does anything that's not good for you. But the things He does do are better than anything you could ever dream!

• •

Lord God, thank You that the things You plan
to give me are even better than I can imagine.

Friends with Jesus

"I call you friends, because I have told you everything I have heard from My Father."
JOHN **15:15**

Friends talk about the things that are important to them, the things that make them happy, the things that worry them. They share secrets. They trust each other to be kind. Real friends aren't bossy. They don't pick on each other. And guess what? Jesus wants to be friends with you! He wants to share with you everything His Father tells Him. He doesn't want you to be His slave or His servant, someone He can boss around. He wants you to be His friend!

• •

Jesus, I'm so glad You want to be friends with me. I want to be a good friend to You too.

Talking to Jesus

*"I will never turn away anyone
who comes to Me."*
JOHN 6:37

When you ask Jesus to be with you, He never says no. Even
if you did something wrong, He never gets mad or holds a
grudge. He's always ready to help you do better. Nothing
is too small to tell Him. He wants you to come to Him and
tell Him everything. And the wonderful thing is—you can
come to Him whenever you want. Right now, before you go
to sleep, and also tomorrow, all throughout the day. Anytime
you want, no matter what you're doing, you can talk to Jesus.
It's like you and Jesus have your own private cell phones,
and you can talk and text whenever you want.

. . . .

*Thank You, Jesus, that You always
listen and You always love me.*

Walls

We have peace because of Christ. . . .
He broke down the wall that divided them.
EPHESIANS 2:14

When you have a fight with a friend or with your brother
or sister, it's like you build a wall between you. That wall is
made of angry feelings and hurt feelings and all kinds of
other upset feelings. The more you think about how angry
you are, and the more you say, "I'm right, and you're wrong!"
the bigger that wall gets.

But you don't have to let those walls get between you and
other people. Jesus wants to knock down all the angry walls
in your life. He wants to bring peace and forgiveness into
your life so that you and others can have fun together again.

* *

Jesus, I'm ready to have You knock down
any walls I've built. I'm ready to stop
being angry and to say I'm sorry.

Tasty, Beautiful God

Taste and see that the Lord is good.
PSALM 34:8

All the things you taste, all your favorite foods, are messages from God. When you bite into an apple or lick an ice cream cone, the taste that fills your mouth is God saying to you, "See how sweet I am? See how good I taste?" When you see something beautiful, like a starry sky or your mother's face, you're getting yet another message from God. He's saying to you, "Look how beautiful I am! See how good I am!" God's goodness is everywhere. You just have to pay attention.

. . . .

*Help me, Lord God, to see Your goodness
in everything I eat and see.*

When Friends Are Mean

Jesus. . .told them in very plain words, saying,
"For sure, I tell you, one of you is going to
hand Me over to the leaders of the country."
JOHN **13:21**

When Jesus was on earth, He had twelve especially close friends. Jesus loved His friends. But one of those friends, Judas, did something to hurt Jesus. Judas got paid a bunch of money to get Jesus in trouble.

Have any of your friends ever been mean to you? Maybe they teased you, or maybe they decided they liked someone else better than you. When something like that happens, it hurts. Jesus understands how you feel. You can tell Him all about it.

. . . .

Jesus, I'm so sorry Your friend was mean to You.
Help me to be a better friend to You than he was.

Empty Cups

"See if I will not. . .pour out good things for you until there is no more need."
MALACHI 3:10

Imagine an empty cup sitting on the table. You're about to pour something into it, maybe juice or something else you like to drink. That's how God wants you to be—ready and waiting for Him to pour good things into your life. Make sure your life isn't so full that you don't have time for God and His blessings. Make lots of room in your life for the wonderful things He wants to give you.

• •

Make my heart like an empty cup, Lord, so that You can fill it with good things.

All Alone

*My God, my God, why have You left me
alone? Why are You so far from helping me,
and from the words I cry inside myself?*
PSALM **22:1**

Sometimes God might let you go through a hard time. You pray, but He doesn't seem to be listening. You ask for His help, but He doesn't seem to do anything. You might feel mad at God. Or you might think you've done something bad that has made God mad at you. Even Jesus had feelings like this when He was dying on the cross. He asked His Father, "Why have You left Me alone?"

But God never *really* leaves you alone. Even when you can't feel Him or see Him, He is with you. He will never, ever leave you. He promised!

* *

*Dear Lord, when I feel like You are far away,
help me to know that You are still with me.*

Sharing the Good News

*Always be ready to tell everyone who
asks you why you believe as you do.*
1 PETER 3:15

Jesus wants you to share the good news about God's love.
This means you talk with others about God the same way
you talk about all the other things in your life. If someone
asks you questions about God, you answer them as best
you can. You're never rude or pushy. You don't act like you
know more or like you're a better person than they are. If
they don't believe the same things you do, God wants you to
respect their beliefs. The most important way you can teach
people about God's love is by always being kind.

* *

*Dear Lord, show me how to share the
good news that You love everyone.*

God's Gifts

*For by His loving-favor you have been
saved from the punishment of sin through
faith. It is not by anything you have
done. It is a gift of God. It is not given
to you because you worked for it.*
EPHESIANS 2:8–9

God's gifts show you that He loves you. They help you feel closer to Him. And His gifts are everywhere, on the inside of you and the outside. We've talked already about all the good things God gives you. God's biggest gifts, though, are Jesus and the Holy Spirit. Jesus came to earth as a baby and became a child who grew up, just like you are growing now, so He understands everything you're going through. He can help you understand God. And through the Holy Spirit, God can live right inside you. What an amazing gift!

* *

*Thank You, Father God, for
everything You have given me.*

In the Fire

*Shadrach, Meshach and Abed-nego. . .said
to the king, "O Nebuchadnezzar. . . If we
are thrown into the fire, our God Whom
we serve is able to save us from it."*
DANIEL 3:16–17

Shadrach, Meshach, and Abednego were living in a country
far from their home. The king wanted them to stop following God. Shadrach, Meshach, and Abednego said, "No, we
are going to do what our God wants us to do. You can do
whatever you want to us, but we trust God." When the king
heard that, he was so mad that he threw the three men into
a huge fire. But when the king looked into the flames, he
was amazed. The three men were just walking around in the
fire. God kept them from being hurt!

*Jesus, thank You that whatever happens
to me, You will be right there with me.*

Three Rules

You must be kind to each other.
Think of the other person. Forgive other
people just as God forgave you.
EPHESIANS **4:32**

Sometimes grown-ups can make following Jesus so complicated! And all along, almost every child has learned the rules the Bible tells us. Rules like the ones listed in this verse from Ephesians:

- Be kind.
- Think how the other person feels.
- Forgive other people when they do something to hurt you.

God wants you to follow these simple rules. And all the while, God is treating you the exact same way! He is always kind to you. He is always thinking about how you feel. And He has forgiven you for all the wrong things you have done.

Thank You, Father, that You are so good to me.

Messages to God

*I love the Lord, because He hears
my voice and my prayers.*
PSALM **116:1**

A hundred years ago, not everyone had a telephone (not even the old-fashioned kind) in their house. If they wanted to talk to a friend, they had to write a letter. It could take weeks before the letter reached their friend. There were no cell phones, no internet, no computers.

Talking to God is a little like texting Him or sending Him an email. You don't have to wait for Him to get the message. You don't have to close your eyes or say special words. You can just say, "Hi," or "I love You," or "Help! I need You!" God is always waiting to hear from you.

• •

*Thank You, Lord, that You get my messages,
no matter where I am or what I'm doing.*

Holy Spirit Power

*The Holy Spirit raised Jesus from the dead.
If the same Holy Spirit lives in you, He will
give life to your bodies in the same way.*
ROMANS **8:11**

No one really understands God. And we don't understand
the Holy Spirit. We know that when we make room inside
us, the Spirit lives there. The Spirit living inside us helps us
love others more. The Spirit comforts us when we're sad
or scared. The Spirit lets us know when we're doing wrong
things. And this Bible verse tells us that the Spirit is also the
one who brought Jesus back to life after He died. That's an
amazing power—power that's bigger and more wonderful
than any superhero has ever had. And when you follow
Jesus, that power lives right inside you!

* *

*Holy Spirit, thank You that Your
wonderful power is inside me.*

Faith

*Now faith is. . .being sure of
what we cannot see.*
HEBREWS 11:1

Imagine you climb a tree and get stuck. Then a grown-up you love and trust climbs up a ladder to help. The grown-up holds out her arms and says, "Drop into my arms. I can catch you."

But you're scared to let go of the tree.

Just believing your grown-up friend isn't going to get you out of that tree. But you know she loves you, and you know her arms are strong. So you let yourself drop—and she catches you and carries you safely to the ground.

That's what faith is like. It's not just believing in God. It's knowing Him, loving Him, and trusting Him enough to give Him your whole life.

• •

Jesus, help my faith in You grow.

Smile for Jesus

"I looked at them with joy when they were not sure of themselves, and the light of my face gave them comfort."
JOB 29:24

You may think you're too young to make a difference in other people's lives. Or you may feel you're too shy to say anything that might help others. But this Bible verse tells us that even a smile is enough to help someone. When someone is feeling scared or worried, your smile could give them courage. Your smile could make a sad person feel a little happier. You might never know it, but your smile could even change someone's life! You're never too young or too shy to smile.

• •

Jesus, I want my smile to help people see You.

Moods

Whatever is good and perfect comes to us from God. . . . He does not change.
JAMES 1:17

We have moods that are always changing. We have good moods when we feel happy. We also have sad moods and angry moods. Sometimes grown-ups' moods can seem downright scary. Your feelings might be hurt when a grown-up snaps at you or scolds you for something little (or for nothing at all). Grown-ups aren't that different from kids, though. Have you ever noticed that when you're tired, you cry more easily? You may also get angry more easily. Grown-ups are the same. When they're tired, they might feel grouchy or sad.

God isn't moody like people are. He's *always* patient and *always* full of joy. He doesn't change.

Thank You, Lord God, that Your love for me never changes.

Sleep

The Lord gives to His loved ones
even while they sleep.
PSALM 127:2

Do you like to go to bed? Or are you a person who hates bedtime, who would stay up all night if you could? Either way, your body needs sleep. While you're asleep, your body is busy taking care of itself. It might even be growing while you sleep! Your body needs sleep in order to be healthy and strong. While you sleep, you dream. It's a little like your brain is telling you stories while you're asleep. And the entire time you're sleeping, God is watching over you. His love is helping your body be healthy and grow. He's even with you in your dreams!

* *

Thank You, Father, that even while I'm
sleeping, You are showing me Your love.

The Wind and the Waves

"Even the winds and the waves obey Him."
MATTHEW 8:27

One day while Jesus and His friends were sailing on the sea, He decided to take a nap. While He was sleeping, a big storm came up and water flooded the boat. The little boat rocked back and forth. Jesus' friends were scared. They thought they might drown. But Jesus was still sleeping! The wind and waves hadn't woken Him. His friends shouted, "Help! We're scared!"

Jesus stood up in the boat. "Stop that," He said to the wind—and the wind stopped. "Calm down," He said to the waves—and the sea became smooth and quiet. Then Jesus turned to His friends. "I was here with you," He said. "So why were you scared?"

• •

Thank You, Jesus, that even when things seem scary, I can relax like You did on the boat.

Happy Right Now

*I have learned to be happy
with whatever I have.*
PHILIPPIANS 4:11

Do you ever think so much about Christmas or summer vacation that you forget to notice the good things you have right now? You have fun toys and games, a comfortable place to live, a family who loves you, and friends who like you—but you're so busy daydreaming about all the fun you'll have when summer vacation comes that you forget to have fun right now. In this verse, the Bible says to you, "Be happy now! God has given you so many wonderful things. Enjoy them!"

• •

*I'm sorry, Lord, if I've been rude to You. Teach
me to be happy with what You give me.*

Love That Never Ends

O give thanks to the Lord, for He is good.
His loving-kindness lasts forever.
1 CHRONICLES 16:34

Imagine a tablecloth that someone has folded up so tight that it looks like a tiny little square. Now picture yourself unfolding the tablecloth, just a little at a time. As you unfold it, the little square gets bigger and bigger. You keep unfolding—and finally, it's so long and wide you have to open the door and take it outside. This is a magic tablecloth, and there will always be more for you to unfold. It will just keep getting wider and longer.

That's what following Jesus is like. Each day you unfold a little more of His love. But no matter how long you live, you will never reach the end of His love. It just keeps getting wider and longer!

. . . .

Thank You, Jesus, that Your love never ends.

Work

Whatever work you do,
do it with all your heart.
COLOSSIANS **3:23**

Grown-ups have jobs—and so do you. A lot of the time, work is fun. Other times, it can be boring or hard. When you feel like that, you might hurry through your work. You might not do as good a job as you could.

Here's something you could try when you don't feel like working: Imagine that the work you are doing is for Jesus. If you're doing homework, picture Jesus instead of your teacher correcting it at school tomorrow. If you're cleaning your room, imagine that Jesus is going to come hang out with you there. That might make you smile—and God will smile right along with you.

• •

Jesus, I want to do all my work for You.

The Bible

"Keep these words of mine in your heart and in your soul."
DEUTERONOMY 11:18

The Bible is full of wonderful promises from God. The more you think about those promises, the more they'll become a part of you. You might even want to memorize some of them so you can always remember them whenever you need them. You could write them on pieces of paper and tape them to your bedroom wall. You could put them inside your schoolbooks, where you'll see them when you're at school or when you do your homework. When you think about what the Bible says, it's like remembering something your favorite person said to you. It makes you feel happy inside.

• •

Thank You, Lord, for all the messages You send me in the Bible.

Be Real

"Be sure you do not do good things in front of others just to be seen by them."
MATTHEW 6:1

God wants you to be kind to other people. He wants you to be His hands and feet, showing people that He loves them. But He doesn't want you to do kind things just so other people will see how good you are. He doesn't want you to fake being kind just so other people will say nice things about you. So when you're nice to someone, don't make a big deal out of it. Don't tell everyone what you did. Let it be a secret between you, God, and the person you were kind to. Make sure your kindness is real.

. . . .

Father God, I want my kindness to be real. I want to show other people how much You love them.

God's Name Is Peace

The Lord is Peace.
JUDGES 6:24

A long time ago, a man named Gideon was a brave leader of the Jewish people. When Gideon's people were in trouble, God sent an angel to talk to him. God wanted Gideon to be brave and stand up against the Jews' enemy. At first, Gideon said to the angel, "I can't do that. I'm too young. I'm too scared."

"God will be with you," the angel told him.

Gideon named the place where they had been talking "The Lord is Peace." He used the word *peace* to mean that God was taking care of everything. From that time on, the place would always remind Gideon that God was with him.

• •

*Thank You, Lord, that You are
taking care of everything.*

Battles

"When you go to battle against those who hate you and see more horses and war-wagons and soldiers than you have, do not be afraid of them. For the Lord your God. . .is with you."
DEUTERONOMY 20:1

You're not going to fight a battle with horses and wagons and soldiers. But you fight other battles every day. You fight the battle to share instead of being selfish. You fight the battle to tell the truth, even when it would be easy to lie. You fight the battle to forgive people when they hurt you. You fight the battle to take time to be nice to someone, even though you'd rather do something else. These are all very important battles to fight. And you can win these battles— because God is with you!

. . . .

Lord God, please fight my battles with me.

God's Map

Teach me Your way, O Lord.
PSALM 27:11

Even thousands of years ago, when King David wrote this verse, people sometimes had a hard time knowing what God wanted them to do. But David knew that even when he wasn't sure what to do, God *always* knew the right way to go. Day by day, God teaches us about Himself and His ways. He shows us how to live. It's like God gives us a map so we don't get lost. All we have to do is follow the directions God gives us—and God will show us His way.

• •

*Father God, when I get mixed up and worried,
help me remember that You are with me
and You are teaching me Your way.*

A Zillion Jillion

*Then Peter. . .said, "Lord, how many times may
my brother sin against me and I forgive him,
up to seven times?" Jesus said to him, "I tell
you, not seven times but seventy times seven!"*
MATTHEW **18:21–22**

What Jesus is really saying in these verses is that forgiveness should have no end. In His day and His language, when He said to forgive seventy times seven, it was like saying, "Forgive a zillion times." A zillion is such a huge number, you can't even count that high. So what Jesus is really saying is this: "Forgive and forgive and forgive. Don't count how many times someone says they're sorry. Just keep on forgiving a zillion jillion times." And that's how many times God will forgive you too!

* *

*Dear Jesus, help me to forgive other people
the same way You always forgive me.*

Alone Time

He went away by Himself to pray.
LUKE 5:16

Even Jesus needed to be alone with God. He talked to His Father all the time throughout the day—just like you can talk to God all through your day, no matter what you're doing—but Jesus still needed times to be quiet and alone. He needed times when nothing would take His attention away from God. He also needed times when He could pay attention to His own thoughts and feelings. Then He could talk to God about everything that was happening. Jesus wants you to copy Him. He wants you to make time to be alone with Him.

• •

Jesus, thank You for showing me how to live.

God's Name

*Those who know Your name
will put their trust in You.*
PSALM 9:10

Long ago, Moses asked God to tell him His name. God said to Moses that His name was "I AM" (Exodus 3:14). That's a strange sort of name, isn't it? Even grown-ups struggle to make sense out of what it means. Here are some ideas about what I AM might mean:

- God is real!
- God is right now! He's not just a memory or something we hope for in the future.
- God is bigger than we can ever imagine.
- God is a mystery, something so big that we will never totally understand Him, even when we go to heaven.

What about you? What do *you* think God's name means?

• •

*Even though I don't understand You,
God, I know You love me.*

Prison

*I want you to know that what has happened
to me has helped spread the Good News.*
PHILIPPIANS 1:12

When the apostle Paul wrote these words, he was in prison.
He wasn't there because he had done anything bad. He had
made people mad, though, by talking about Jesus. Paul
might have felt angry and frustrated. It wasn't fair that he
was in jail. He might have felt sad and discouraged. But Paul
trusted God to take care of everything. And things turned
out just fine. In prison, Paul spent a lot of time talking to
the guards about Jesus. The guards decided they wanted
to follow Jesus too. They went home and told their families
and friends about Jesus. Pretty soon the whole city knew
the story of Jesus!

* *

*Jesus, help me be like Paul. I know
You will work everything out.*

Staying Close to God

Learn to pray about everything.
PHILIPPIANS 4:6

Imagine a good friend you talk to every day. Now imagine you move to a new town and a new school. Your friend and you promise to stay friends—but soon you forget to message her. You don't call her on the phone anymore. Now you don't know what's going on in her life—and she doesn't know what's happening in yours. Pretty soon she's not your close friend anymore.

The same thing can happen with God. If you never talk to Him, you won't feel close to Him. You won't learn what He wants to tell you. That's why the Bible says to pray about everything all the time.

* *

*Thank You, Lord God, that I can
talk to You anytime I want.*

No Fighting Allowed

Jesus said. . ."Put your sword
back where it belongs."
MATTHEW 26:52

Jesus hadn't done anything wrong, but soldiers were going to arrest Him and take Him away. One of Jesus' friends, Peter, jumped up and pulled out a sword. He wanted to protect Jesus. But Jesus told him, "Don't do that. Don't hurt anyone because of Me."

You probably aren't going to pull out a sword to fight. We do live in a world where people fight each other, though. But Jesus wants you to be different from the rest of the world. He doesn't want you to shove or hit or hurt people. Instead of fighting, He wants you to show everyone how much He loves them.

• •

Jesus, help me to do my part to fill
the world with Your love.

A Great Full Life

*"I came so they might have
life, a great full life."*
John 10:10

Sometimes people think that following Jesus means you're
not allowed to have any fun. But that's not the way it is at
all. Jesus says in this verse that He came so you could have
even *more* fun. He came so your life could be bigger and
better, full of all sorts of wonderful things. Sure, there are
things He doesn't want you to do, but His rules are meant
to keep you safe because He loves you so much. He knows
what will really make you happiest and healthiest. He wants
you to have a great life!

* *

*Thank You, Jesus, that You promise to
give me a full and wonderful life!*

Showers of Blessing

"Good will rain down upon them."
EZEKIEL **34:26**

Have you ever heard people talk about "showers of blessing"? It's a saying that comes from this verse. It means that when God pours out good things on you, it's like the rain falling on the earth. Not everyone likes rainy days—but the earth needs rain. Without rain, plants couldn't grow. Farmers wouldn't be able to grow food. Pretty soon everything would look dry and brown, like a desert. And it's the same way with the good things God sends into your life. Those good things give you life. They help you grow. They make your life beautiful. And they give you what you need to help other people too.

• •

Thank You, Father, that You are always pouring good things into my life.

Promises

It is better not to make a promise,
than to make a promise and not pay it.
ECCLESIASTES 5:5

Has a friend ever told you something like this: "If you give me your cookies, I promise you I'll give you candy tomorrow"? So you let your friend have your cookies—but when the next day comes, he doesn't give you any candy. How do you feel when people break their promises? It doesn't feel good, does it? Sometimes people really mean to keep their promises, but something happens so they can't. That's why the Bible says it's better not to make promises unless you're absolutely sure you can keep those promises.

· ·

Thank You, Lord, that You always
keep Your promises.

Teasing

Do not let kindness and truth leave
you. Tie them around your neck.
Write them upon your heart.
PROVERBS 3:3

Children like to tease each other. They like to make fun of each other. Sometimes even grown-ups like to tease. Teasing can be fun—but a lot of the time it can hurt your feelings. The other person might not have meant to hurt you, but it doesn't feel nice to have everyone laughing at you. If you don't like when people tease you, be careful not to join in when someone else is being teased. The Bible says to tie kindness around your neck like a scarf. Write it on your heart so you never forget it.

. . . .

Jesus, help me always to be kind.

Prayer and Joy

Be full of joy all the time. Never stop praying. In everything give thanks. This is what God wants you to do because of Christ Jesus. Do not try to stop the work of the Holy Spirit.
1 THESSALONIANS 5:16–19

The Bible tells you:

- Bc full of joy all the time.
- Never stop praying.
- Give thanks in everything.
- Don't get in the way of what the Holy Spirit is doing.

It all comes down to letting the Holy Spirit work in your life. When you let Him do what He wants, you trust that God is always doing what is best, and you tell Him thank You. You might not be talking to God every minute, but you're always ready to hear His voice. Living this way will make you happy.

* *

Holy Spirit, thank You for what You are doing in my life.

Worrying

*"Which of you can make himself
a little taller by worrying?"*
MATTHEW 6:27

What kinds of things do you worry about? Maybe you worry
that other kids don't like you. You might worry that you don't
have the same kind of shoes that everyone else in your class
has. Everyone worries sometimes—but worry never, ever
does any good. It doesn't make things turn out the way we
want. As Jesus is saying in this verse, you could worry all
day about being short, but worrying would never make you
grow an inch! Worrying is just a waste of time. It makes us
unhappy without doing us any good. It's far better to trust
God to take care of everything!

* *

*I give You all my worries, Father God,
the big ones and the little ones.*

Angels

*"At that time the great angel Michael,
who watches over your people, will rise up."*
DANIEL 12:1

Angels are real. We don't know what they look like, but they probably don't have big wings like they do in pictures. In the Bible, angels usually look like people except they shine or they're dressed all in white. The Bible also describes crazy-looking creatures that are covered with wings and eyes or have four faces. What we do know about angels is that they are God's messengers and God's fighters. Angels watch over people and fight evil. Jesus even says we each have our own angels (Matthew 18:10). Angels are just one more way God sends His love out into the world!

* *

*Thank You, Lord, that Your
angels watch over me.*

Giving

"We are more happy when we give than when we receive."
ACTS 20:35

At Christmastime, which do you like better: opening your own presents or watching your family open the presents you gave them? We all get excited about presents, but Jesus wants you to learn that giving to people truly will make you happier than getting things from people. When you give, you are being like God, who gives and gives and gives—and never expects to get anything back from us in return. When you give, you are saying you don't want to be selfish or put yourself first. When you give, you show people you love them. You'll find out that giving makes you happy!

• •

Teach me to be like You, Lord. Teach me to give.

Great Big God

"Am I a God Who is near," says the Lord,
"and not a God Who is far away? Can
a man hide himself in secret places so
that I cannot see him?" says the Lord.
JEREMIAH **23:23–24**

If you were trying to play hide-and-seek with God, He would find you every time. There's no hiding place so tiny that He couldn't see you there. And not only would He see you, but He would crawl right into your hiding place with you! God says He is close beside you even when you're hiding from everyone else. But at the same time, God fills the entire world, including outer space. This great big God loves you so much that He'll do anything just to be with you!

Great big God, thank You that
You are always with me.

Arguing and Complaining

Do all things without arguing and talking about how you wish you did not have to do them.
PHILIPPIANS 2:14

When a grown-up tells you to do something, what do you do? Suppose your mom says you have to clean your room. But you really want to go to a friend's house to play. Do you go clean your room and do a good job—or do you argue with your mom? God wants you to do what you're asked without arguing or complaining. Having a good attitude shows your mom you love her and respect her. It shows God that you love Him too!

• •

Dear Father God, when I don't feel like doing something, help me to do it anyway, without making a fuss.

Love Circles

"Respect and give thanks for those who try to bring bad to you. Pray for those who make it very hard for you."
LUKE 6:28

When someone does something mean to you, instead of doing something even meaner back, be nice. Pray for the person who was mean to you. Do something kind for them. When you do that, you put an end to a circle where everyone is doing mean things to each other, one after another. You create a new kind of circle instead. When you're nice to someone, they're more likely to be nice to you too. When you help people see that Jesus loves them, ugly circles stop—and love circles begin.

• •

Jesus, when someone is mean to me, help me to love them the way You do.

Prayer Time

You must be the boss over your mind.
Keep awake so you can pray.
1 PETER 4:7

Did you know you can be the boss over your own mind? That means you don't have to let your thoughts run all over the place when you're trying to pray. Of course tonight, if you're sleepy, God doesn't expect you to stay awake praying. But when you are praying, He wants you to pay attention to Him. He doesn't want you to be thinking about what you're going to do tomorrow or daydreaming about something else. If you're talking to someone and you can tell they're not really paying attention to you, you start to feel frustrated, don't you? So don't do that to God!

. . . .

I love You, Jesus, and I want to
spend time with You.

No More Frowns!

"I will put off my sad face and be happy."
Job 9:27

Things don't always go the way you want, do they? Maybe you were hoping to go do something fun—but instead your parents have to work. You could spend the whole day being sad and disappointed. You could complain and whine, making everyone around you miserable too. But you don't have to do that. You have a choice. You can choose to enjoy the day anyway. You stop thinking about what you wanted to do, and you find something different to do. You take off your frown and put on a smile. When you do that, you'll find that things aren't so bad after all!

• •

When I feel sad and disappointed, Lord, help me to remember that I can choose to smile anyway.

God Chose You

*God has chosen you. You are
holy and loved by Him.*
COLOSSIANS **3:12**

Have you ever been the last kid to be picked for a team?
When all your friends were going to a birthday party, did
you not get an invitation? Not being chosen to be a part of
something hurts. It makes you feel left out and forgotten.
But that will never happen with God. He chose *you*. Sure,
He loves everyone—but His love for you is special. No one
else in the whole world can be friends with God in the exact
same way you can. No one else can do the job He's given you
to do, because no one else can show God's love the same
way you can. God needs the one and only you!

. . . .

Lord God, thank You so much for choosing me.

Jesus Understands

Christ was tempted in every way we
are tempted, but He did not sin.
HEBREWS 4:15

Jesus remembers what it was like to be young, and He knows what you're feeling. When you feel like being selfish, He understands. He gets it when you feel sad or angry or scared. But the big difference with Jesus is this—even though He had all those feelings, He never let anything come between Him and His Father. So now He knows how to help you do the right thing. You never have to feel ashamed or embarrassed or shy about telling Him anything. He understands exactly how you feel.

* *

Jesus, thank You that You understand
what it's like to be a kid.

Sharing

"Is it not a time to share your food with the hungry, and bring the poor man into your house who has no home of his own? Is it not a time to give clothes to the person you see who has no clothes?"
ISAIAH **58:7**

God wants you to share whatever you have with others. There are all kinds of ways to share. You might share your lunch with someone who doesn't have a lunch. You might also share in a bigger way. For example, you could go through all your toys and pick out ones to give away to children who don't have toys. When you put money in the offering plate at church, that's a way to share too. Sometimes sharing just means taking time to be nice to someone.

• •

Father God, please help me not to be selfish.

Count Your Blessings

You make him glad with the joy of being with You.
PSALM 21:6

At night while you're falling asleep is a good time to make a list in your head of all the ways God showed you He loves you today. Your list might be something like this:

- I had fun playing with my dog.
- I liked talking to my mom tonight.
- We had my favorite food for dinner.
- I love the book I'm reading.
- I'm happy I get to visit my grandma this weekend.
- The flowers I picked today were beautiful.

You'll have your own list, of course. God shows His love in lots of different ways!

* *

Thank You, Lord, for how happy You make me every day.

A Different Way of Acting

"I tell you, love those who hate you."
MATTHEW 5:44

If someone isn't very nice to you, you don't usually want to be nice to them. You pray for people who have been kind to you—but why would you want to pray for people who are mean to you? You say hello to your friends—but why would you say hello to people you don't like? But Jesus turns everything around. "Show My love to *everyone*," He says. "Be nice to *everyone*. It doesn't matter whether they're mean to you or you don't like them. Don't act like everyone else! Show people My love."

. . . .

Jesus, help me be more like You.

Carried in God's Arms

"The Lord your God carried you."
DEUTERONOMY 1:31

Have you ever heard a poem called "Footprints in the Sand"? The poem often shows a picture of the beach with just one set of footprints in the sand. The story behind the picture and poem is about someone going for a walk with God. A storm comes and everything gets dark. When the person looks back, she sees just one set of footprints. "Why did You leave me all alone during the storm?" she asks God.

"Those aren't your footprints," God tells her. "They're Mine. I was carrying you."

When you feel too small or scared to keep following Jesus, God picks you up and carries you in His arms.

· ·

Thank You, Father, that when I'm tired and weak, Your arms are strong enough to carry me.

God Made You Just Right!

*I will give thanks to You. . . . Your works
are great and my soul knows it very well.*
PSALM **139:14**

People often feel as if they have to be like everyone else. And when they see that they're not like everyone else, that they're different in some way, they think something is wrong with them. Is there anything about yourself you don't like? God loves you just the way you are! He doesn't want you to compare yourself to other people. He wants you to just enjoy being you, the special person He made you to be. He wants you to love *you*!

• •

Father God, thank You for making me special.

Nature

"In His hand is the life of every living thing."
JOB 12:10

The Bible is an important way you can get to know God. You can also get to know Him better by learning from people who have been following Jesus for a long time. You can get to know God just by spending time with Him, talking to Him. And the Bible says that nature can help you know God too. When you learn about wild animals, when you watch birds flying, when you plant a garden, when you see the fish in the ocean, these are all chances to learn more about God. Pay attention to the beautiful world God has made!

* *

*Thank You, Lord God, for making
our beautiful world.*

What Is God Like?

Those who do not love do not know
God because God is love.
1 JOHN 4:8

When people know you are following God, they might have some questions. Will you be able to answer them? Here are some ideas that will help:

- God made everything—the sun, moon, and stars, the earth, the animals and plants, and you and me.
- God loves all the things He made. He loves you and me.
- God shows His love to us in lots of ways. He made a beautiful world. He sent Jesus to us. He fills our lives with good things.
- God takes care of us. We can talk to Him about our lives, and He listens.
- God always loves. Everything He does comes from His love.

What else would *you* say about God?

. . . .

Show me how to tell people about You, Lord.

Garbage

"See, it was for my own well-being that I was bitter."
ISAIAH 38:17

"Why do you throw our garbage into a pile?" a child asked her dad.

"Because," her dad said, "that garbage—all the eggshells and potato peelings and apple cores—will turn into dirt. And that dirt will make the tomato plants in our garden grow tall and healthy next summer."

"But it smells yucky."

"Yes, it does," her dad agreed. "But it's full of good stuff that will feed the garden."

Sometimes stuff in our lives seems yucky—but it is really helping us grow. God uses everything to build His kingdom of love, even the parts of our lives that seem like garbage!

• •

When my life seems full of garbage,
Lord, help me to remember that You can
use everything to help me grow.

Time Away

[Jesus] said to [His followers], "Come away from the people. Be by yourselves and rest."
MARK 6:31

Jesus and His friends had busy lives. They didn't just sit around doing nothing. They traveled around telling people the good news that God loved them. But Jesus also knew when He needed to take some time away. He knew He and His friends needed to get away and just be together sometimes.

Do you have a busy life? Is your schedule full of after-school activities? Is your family so busy you often don't have time to eat dinner together? You might need some time out from being busy. Maybe you could find a time to be like Jesus and His friends—a time to go away and just enjoy being together.

. . . .

Jesus, help me never to be too busy to spend time with others and with You.

Your Job

*The Spirit of the Lord God is on me,
because the Lord has chosen me to bring
good news to poor people. He has sent
me to heal those with a sad heart.*
ISAIAH **61:1**

Jesus said, "This verse from the book of Isaiah is about Me. My job is to bring good news to people who are poor. My job is to help sick people be well and sad people be happy" (see Luke 4:16–21). *You* can do the same thing Jesus did—you can take this verse and say, "This is about *me*. This is my job too. My job is to let the Holy Spirit use me to tell people that God loves them. My job is to help people however I can. I probably can't make sick people healthy—but I can help sad people be happy."

. . . .

*Help me, Jesus, to do my job by telling people
the good news of Your love for them.*

First and Last

*"I am the First and the Last. I am
the beginning and the end."*
REVELATION 22:13

What do you think Jesus meant when He said, "I am first
and I am last, the beginning and the end"? He might have
meant He was there at the very beginning of the world,
and He will be there when the world comes to an end. He
might also mean that just as He was there when you were a
brand-new baby, He will be with you when you're very, very
old. And Jesus might also mean that absolutely everything
in the whole world is His. Nothing is too small or too big
for His love and care.

* *

*Jesus, thank You that my whole life
belongs to You, from beginning to end.*

God Stories

O Lord, You are my God. I will praise
You. I will give thanks to Your name.
ISAIAH 25:1

God's special people, the Jews, liked to remember all the things God had done for them. When things were hard, they told each other the stories of all the ways God had helped them in the past. They loved to hear those stories over and over because the stories helped them remember how strong God is and how much He loved them. What stories could you tell? What is something God has done for you? What do you like to remember about God? As you go to sleep tonight, you might like to tell yourself those stories. They'll help you remember how much God loves you.

* *

You have done so many good things for me,
Lord God. Help me to remember them all.

Roots and Branches

Have your roots planted deep in Christ.
COLOSSIANS 2:7

A tree grows very slowly. Sometimes its trunk and branches might not change very much—but down under the ground, where you can't see, the tree's roots are growing deeper and deeper. Without deep roots, the tree could not grow tall. God wants you to have strong "roots" too. This means your friendship with Him grows and grows. This friendship happens inside you, where no one else can see, but as time goes by, people will be able to see more and more clearly that you and Jesus are friends. The love you and Jesus share is the roots. The way you show your love to others is the branches.

* *

Jesus, may my friendship with You grow and grow inside me—so that I can show Your love to everyone on the outside.

Bread Dough and Heaven

*"The holy nation of heaven is like yeast that
a woman put into three pails of flour until
it had become much more than at first."*
MATTHEW 13:33

In this verse, Jesus says heaven is like the yeast in bread. Yeast is what makes bread rise. If a little ball of bread dough is in a bowl, the yeast that's inside the dough will make the dough get bigger and bigger. It might even spill over the edges of the bowl! Jesus says the kingdom of heaven is like that. It can start very small, but then it grows and grows. The kingdom of heaven Jesus is talking about is God's kingdom of heaven right here, right now. So many things in our world are sad and bad—but don't worry. God's kingdom is here too. And it's *growing*!

. . . .

*Thank You, Jesus, that Your kingdom is
growing around me and inside me.*

God's Plans

"For I know the plans I have for you," says the
Lord, "plans for well-being and not for trouble."
JEREMIAH **29:11**

Do you ever feel scared of the future? Especially if something
bad has happened, you may be scared something like that
will happen again. You may worry about what it will be like
to be a grown-up one day. You might even worry sometimes
about dying. But you don't have to worry about any of those
things. God has plans for you, plans to give you hope and
a bright future. He plans to use everything that will ever
happen to you to bring you closer to Him. So why be scared?

· ·

Thank You, Father God, that You have
plans for me, plans for a beautiful life that
will lead me closer and closer to You.

Stop Wiggling!

"The Lord will fight for you.
All you have to do is keep still."
EXODUS 14:14

Has someone who was cutting your hair ever said to you, "Sit still. Don't move!"? It's hard not to wiggle when hair is tickling your neck and eyes. You might even worry that the haircutter's scissors will slip and cut you. Wiggling doesn't help, though. It just makes it harder for the haircutter to do his job. You have to hold still and trust him not to hurt you. Sometimes God might be saying the same thing to you—"Hold still—stop wiggling! Trust Me. I know what I'm doing!"

* *

Dear Lord, please teach me to be still
and to trust You. Thank You that You are
taking care of everything in my life.

The Holy Spirit

*While He was praying that good would
come to them, He went from them
(*and was taken up to heaven).*
LUKE 24:51

Right in the middle of praying for His friends, Jesus left them and went to be with His Father. Imagine how you would have felt if you had been one of Jesus' friends watching Him disappear! Would you have been scared? Excited? Sad? Jesus knew how His friends would feel. That's why He sent His Spirit to be with His friends, even when they could no longer see Him. The Holy Spirit lived right inside them, helping them. And the same Holy Spirit is still with us today!

* *

*Thank You, Holy Spirit, that You
never leave me all alone.*

When You're Sick

Be kind to me, O Lord, for I am weak.
O Lord, heal me for my bones are shaken.
PSALM 6:2

It's hard to be happy when you're sick. Sometimes being sick hurts a lot, and it can be scary. Jesus understands all those feelings. When He was on earth, He healed all sorts of sicknesses. Jesus still heals sickness. He helps your body get better and heal. Sometimes He uses doctors and medicines to make you well. And while you're waiting to get better, He's right there with you. Being sick is a good chance to spend more time talking to Him.

• •

When I'm sick, Jesus, help me to
remember that You are with me.

Time

I say, "You are my God."
My times are in Your hands.
PSALM 31:14–15

Do you ever wish you could do whatever you want *whenever* you want? When your parents tell you it's time to get up in the morning, do you wish you could roll over and hide your head under your pillow? And then when night comes and your parents say it's bedtime, do you wish they would let you play as long as you liked? God wants you to remember that all time belongs to Him. Every minute of every day and night is His. When you trust your time to God, you stop wanting to do whatever you want when *you* want. You give every hour and minute to Him.

* *

Father God, I give You my playtime,
chore time, schooltime, after-school
time, bedtime, and getting-up time.

Brand New

"Do not be surprised that I said to you, 'You must be born again.'"
JOHN 3:7

When it was time for you to be born, you didn't say, "Okay, Mom, I've decided I'm ready to be born now, so I'm coming on out." When Jesus says you need to be born again, He doesn't mean you have to go back inside your mother's stomach—and He also doesn't mean you have to work hard to be good. He means He will give you a brand-new way to live. You will become a brand-new person. All you have to do is spend time with Him and follow Him. He'll do the rest.

. . . .

Jesus, thank You that You have given me a brand-new life with You.

Wonderful Things Ahead!

"No eye has ever seen or no ear has ever heard or no mind has ever thought of the wonderful things God has made ready for those who love Him."
1 CORINTHIANS 2:9

You don't ever have to worry or be scared about something that will happen tomorrow, next week, next year, or even years and years from now when you're all grown up. God was with you in the past, He's with you right now, and He's already up ahead in the future, getting things ready for you. You don't know what will happen, but you do know God loves you. And because He loves you, He has wonderful things planned for you!

· ·

Father God, thank You that You are making a wonderful tomorrow ready for me.

Life Jacket

My soul goes to You to be safe.
PSALM 57:1

God never promises that bad things won't happen in your life—but He does promise He'll be with you always. In a way, God is like a life jacket. If you were out in the ocean in the middle of a storm, you might drown. But if you were wearing a life jacket, it would help to keep you safe. The wind and the waves would still be blowing and tossing. They wouldn't magically go away just because you have a life jacket. The waves might still throw you back and forth—but so long as you keep your life jacket on, you won't drown. The life jacket will keep you from sinking.

* *

Thank You, Lord God, that You are my life jacket.

Caterpillars and Butterflies

*All the time we are being changed
to look like Him, with more and
more of His shining-greatness.*
2 CORINTHIANS 3:18

A caterpillar is a creepy-crawly thing. It can't move very fast. It's not really all that pretty. But one day, that caterpillar turns into a butterfly. It's like magic. The slow, crawly thing now has beautiful wings. It can flutter and fly.

Did you know you are a little like a caterpillar? No, you're not a creepy-crawly—but something amazing is happening to you. As you follow Jesus, you are being changed, just like the caterpillar changed. You are starting to look and act like Jesus. And one day you will even shine like Jesus!

• •

*I'm so glad, Jesus, that You are helping
me to grow more like You.*

Make Things Right

"If you take your gift to the altar and remember your brother has something against you, leave your gift on the altar. Go and make right what is wrong between you and him. Then come back and give your gift."
MATTHEW 5:23–24

In this verse, Jesus is talking about saying you're sorry after you've hurt someone. He's saying, "Don't try to talk to Me and tell Me all the things you're going to do for Me—not if you've hurt someone. Before you can do anything else for Me, you need to make things right with the person you hurt. Go say you're sorry. Ask what you can do to help the other person feel better. And *then* come back and spend time with Me."

* *

Jesus, help me to be brave and loving enough to say I'm sorry.

Waiting for God

The eyes of all look to You.
PSALM 145:15

Waiting seems like such a waste of time. It seems like time that could be spent doing something better. Waiting feels empty and boring. When you're waiting for something, it can feel like you'll *never* get it.

But God wants you and me to learn to be patient. He wants us to treasure each moment, because there is never an empty moment when He is not with us. Even time that seems wasted or boring can be time spent with God. While we wait, we can talk to God. And at the right time, our wait will be over!

• •

Father God, show me how to keep my eyes on You, even when I'm waiting and bored.

The Invisible World

Christ is as God is. God cannot be seen.
Christ lived before anything was made.
COLOSSIANS 1:15

People have a hard time believing in what they can't see. Grown-ups especially seem to have a hard time with this. They think that if they can't see something or touch something, it must not be real. They think that invisible things must be imaginary. But scientists have found out the world is full of very real things that we can't see. Our world is full of mystery, wonderful things that are hard to understand—but are *real*. And God is the most mysterious, most wonderful, most real thing of all!

· ·

Lord God, even though I can't see You or
touch You, I'm so glad You are real!

Disappointment

*Hope never makes us ashamed because
the love of God has come into our hearts
through the Holy Spirit Who was given to us.*
ROMANS 5:5

Disappointed is how you feel when you wanted something to happen—but it didn't. Maybe you had wished for a certain video game for Christmas—but instead you got a game you already have. Maybe you thought dinner would be your favorite meal—and it turned out to be the food you dislike the most.

Many times, people in the Bible were also disappointed. But even when things didn't turn out the way they wanted, they still had hope. They knew God would work everything out. They trusted Him.

* *

*Thank You, Lord, that You will
always do what's best for me.*

Family Problems

*For my father and my mother have left
me. But the Lord will take care of me.*
PSALM **27:10**

Families can be wonderful. Your family teaches you how to love and be loved. Your family is one of the special gifts God gave you. But sometimes families hurt each other. They get in fights and say mean things. Sometimes people in families get sick, and then they can't do all the things they want. Or they are too busy. Even if your family isn't there for you when you need them, God will be there. He is never mean, never sick, never too busy. He will never, ever let you down.

· ·

*Father God, when my family has problems,
please help us. Teach us how to get along better.*

Bread from Heaven

Then the Lord said to Moses, "See, I will rain bread from heaven for you."
EXODUS 16:4

God's people, the Jews, had been made into slaves. God sent Moses to lead them to freedom—and he did. But after the people were free, they found themselves wandering around in the desert. They didn't have anything to eat, and they were hungry.

So God made a kind of bread fall from the sky. It was sweet like honey, and the people could eat all they wanted. They weren't hungry anymore. God had taken care of them after all.

• •

Lord God, when I start to think You aren't going to help me, remind me not to give up.

Sad Days

*Why are you sad, O my soul? . . . Hope in God,
for I will yet praise Him, my help and my God.*
PSALM **42:11**

Sad days come to everyone. Days when nothing seems to go right. Days when you feel lonely, when it seems like no one understands you. Days when you wonder if anyone *really* loves you. When you have one of those days, remember God is doing good things in your life, even right now. Sad feelings can make the world seem like a bad place, but feelings are just feelings. They never last for very long. Sad feelings come and go, but God's love is always the same.

* *

*When I feel sad, dear Lord, help
me remember that You are doing
something wonderful right now.*

More Than You Need

God can give you all you need.
He will give you more than enough.
2 Corinthians 9:8

The Bible has a lot of good advice about selfishness. This verse says that one way you can stop being selfish is to remember that God has given you everything you need. All the wonderful things in your life aren't really *yours*. They belong to God, but He lets you use them all. Because He shares everything with you, you have more than enough for yourself. You'll always have enough to share. You'll have enough to help someone who needs help.

* *

Help me, Lord, not to be selfish. Help me to share everything You've given me, the same way You've shared everything with me.

Jesus Shows Us the Father

"Whoever has seen Me, has seen the Father."
JOHN **14:9**

One reason Jesus came to live with us on earth was to show us God. Jesus is God, but He is also a human being like you and me. If you want to know what God is like, read about Jesus in the Bible. See how Jesus acts. See how He treats people. See the way He talks. Find out for yourself what Jesus is like. That way, if someone tells you something about God that doesn't seem like Jesus, you'll be able to see they're wrong. Really get to know Jesus, and you'll get to know God.

* *

Jesus, I want to get to know You better.

The Kingdom of God

Jesus said. . . "The holy nation of God is not coming in such a way that can be seen with the eyes."
LUKE 17:20

When Jesus was on earth, He spoke often about God's kingdom. Sometimes Jesus called it the kingdom of heaven. He was talking about a special world that's all around us right now—God's kingdom. God's kingdom is a world where His love rules. It's a world where everyone does what's right, and nothing is broken or ugly. We can't see this world yet—but it's real! Jesus tried to help us understand God's kingdom by using word pictures. He said, "God's kingdom is like a seed that starts out small and then grows bigger. God's kingdom is like buried treasure. It's like a party." And He said, "God's kingdom is inside *you*!"

. . . .

Show me, Jesus, how I can be a part of God's kingdom.

Getting Even

"Do not hurt someone who has hurt you. . .but love your neighbor as yourself."
LEVITICUS 19:18

Have you ever been so mad at a friend that you decided you weren't going to speak to him until he said he was sorry? Or when someone teased you and made you feel bad, did you tease her back so she'd feel bad too? That might seem fair—but the Bible says you should treat others the way you would like to be treated. This means when you feel hurt, you don't try to get even. In God's kingdom, there is no getting even. Two people both being mean will never make things fair. Hurting people is never the answer. Showing love is!

• •

When my feelings are hurt, Lord, help me to forgive others the way You forgive me.

177

Big Ideas

Then Peter said to Jesus, "Lord, it is good for us to be here. If You will let us, we will build three altars here."
MATTHEW 17:4

One day, Peter saw Jesus talking to two men, Moses and Elijah—even though both men had been dead for hundreds of years! Moses and Elijah weren't ghosts. They were alive! And Jesus was shining! Peter was so excited that he shouted something like this: "I've got an idea! Let's build three tabernacles here, one for You, Jesus, and one for Moses and one for Elijah." But God didn't want Peter to build a tabernacle or make an altar. A voice from the cloud said, "This is My much-loved Son. . . . Listen to Him!" (Matthew 17:5).

* *

When I get excited about a big idea, Jesus, remind me to check it out with You and see what You think.

Since You Were Young

You are my hope, O Lord God.
PSALM 71:5

David, who wrote most of the book of Psalms in the Bible, was friends with God ever since he was a boy. During David's lifetime, he fought a giant. He became king. He did good things, and he did bad things—but he always came back to God and asked for His help. David spent so many years following God that he got to know God very well. He knew that the same God who had been with him since he was a boy taking care of sheep would *always* be with him.

. . . .

*Thank You, Lord, that I will get to know
You better and better all through my life.*

Tests

Dear friends, your faith is going to be tested as if it were going through fire. Do not be surprised at this. Be happy that you are able to share some of the suffering of Christ. When His shining-greatness is shown, you will be filled with much joy.
1 PETER 4:12–13

When a teacher gives you a test at school, he wants to find out how much you've learned. Sometimes when you have to face something hard in your life (something sad or scary), it can be like a test. Can you trust God even when life is hard? Have you learned how much He *really* loves you—or do you still need to learn more about God? Don't worry. This isn't the kind of test you can flunk! God will be with you no matter what.

• •

*Jesus, when hard times come,
help me to turn to You.*

Forever Life

Jesus said. . ."I am the One Who raises the dead and gives them life. Anyone who puts his trust in Me will live again, even if he dies."
JOHN 11:25

Death is hard to understand. When someone you love dies, it's very sad. You miss that person. You wish you could be with them again. But Jesus doesn't want you to be afraid of death. He came to tell you that when you follow Him, you will never *really* die. Even when your body dies, the inside part of you (who you *really* are!) will live on with God. Jesus died on the cross, but then He came back to life. You will too! The life Jesus gives will last forever.

. . . .

Thank You, Jesus, that because You live in my heart, I will live with You forever.

Runaway Thoughts

*We take hold of every thought
and make it obey Christ.*
2 CORINTHIANS 10:5

Have you ever tried to pray—and two minutes later found out you're actually daydreaming? Or have you tried to pray about angry feelings—only to find that instead of talking to Jesus and asking for help, you're right back to thinking about how angry you are? When you notice your thoughts are running away, you can grab hold of them and give them to God. You might have to do that ten times or a hundred times. It doesn't matter how many times you have to do it. You just keep doing it. Remember, your thoughts aren't the boss!

• •

*Jesus, when my thoughts try to run away, help
me to grab them and give them to You.*

Joy

"We will have joy and be glad because of you."
SONG OF SOLOMON **1:4**

Following Jesus should make you smile more and sing more. If it doesn't, something is wrong. Jesus doesn't want His followers to be sad, frowny people who never laugh and never have fun. The Bible is full of verses about the joy that God gives. Here are just three:

- "Joy that lasts forever will crown their heads. They will be glad and full of joy. Sorrow and sad voices will be gone" (Isaiah 35:10).
- "I will have joy in the Lord. I will be glad in the God Who saves me" (Habakkuk 3:18).
- "Let all who put their trust in You be glad. Let them sing with joy forever" (Psalm 5:11).

• •

Thank You, Father God, for the joy You give me!

Second Chances

*God Who began the good work in
you will keep on working in you until
the day Jesus Christ comes again.*
PHILIPPIANS 1:6

Jonah is someone in the Bible who found it hard to trust God. When God told Jonah to go preach to the city of Nineveh, Jonah said no. He ran away from God. You probably know what happened next. He ended up in the stomach of a great fish, all because he didn't trust God. But God didn't leave Jonah. He gave Jonah a second chance, and this time, Jonah did what God told him to do.

Even when you don't listen to God, He's right there with you. He'll give you another chance to follow Him.

. . . .

Thank You, Lord, for another chance.

Learn from Jesus

*"Follow My teachings and learn from
Me. I am gentle and do not have pride.
You will have rest for your souls."*
MATTHEW **11:29**

When Jesus was on earth, He didn't need to be the strongest
or most important. He didn't go around yelling, "I'm the Son
of God, so give me everything I want!" He was gentle and
kind. And that's how He wants you to be too. He wants you
to stop caring whether you're first or last, best or worst. All
He wants you to care about is helping others and showing
them that God loves them.

*Jesus, when I feel mad or sad that I'm
not the best or the most important,
help me to be more like You.*

Nothing!

Who can keep us away from the love of Christ? Can trouble or problems? Can suffering wrong from others or having no food? Can it be because of no clothes or because of danger or war? . . . I know that nothing can keep us from the love of God. Death cannot! Life cannot! Angels cannot! Leaders cannot! Any other power cannot! Hard things now or in the future cannot! The world above or the world below cannot! Any other living thing cannot keep us away from the love of God which is ours through Christ Jesus our Lord.
ROMANS 8:35, 38–39

God loves you! And absolutely nothing can come between you and God's love.

• •

Jesus, when I feel sad or scared, help me to remember that You won't let anything come between me and You.

Learning

Teach me Your way, O Lord.
I will walk in Your truth.
PSALM 86:11

No matter how many times you make a mistake, God never gets mad. He is patient and gentle with you. He gives you time to learn about Him and His love. Even when you're slow to learn—maybe because you're being stubborn or because you haven't been paying attention—God never gives up on you. Little by little, you learn more and more. It will take time. But you don't have to wait until you're older to know God. You can begin to learn from Him now. While you're still a kid, you and God can be friends.

. . . .

Father God, I want to know You
better and better each day.

Comfort

He gives us comfort in all our troubles.
Then we can comfort other people
who have the same troubles.
2 Corinthians 1:4

The bed where you're going to sleep tonight is comfortable—it's a soft, warm place to lie. Your favorite pajamas are comfortable. They don't itch or scratch, and they're not too tight or too small. God gives you that kind of comfort, making you feel safe and warm, like everything is just right. Comfort is also something God gives you when you're sad. He helps you feel better and takes the sad feelings away. And just like everything in God's kingdom, comfort is something He wants you to share.

• •

Thank You, Lord, for showing me how
to comfort other people so that they
will see how much You love them.

Rae Simons has been writing for Barbour Books for almost thirty years. She lives in New York State with her family and her many well-loved animals.

More Bedtime Bible Inspiration for Kids!

365 Best-Loved Bedtime Bible Stories for Kids

Beginning with the creation story, "God Creates the Earth," and ending with "In Eternity with God," your children will develop faith in an almighty God who is the same yesterday, today, and forever, while journeying alongside Bible characters like Samuel, Jonah, Esther, David, John the Baptist, Mary, Joseph, and many more. *365 Best-Loved Bedtime Bible Stories for Kids* promises to make bedtime reading a delightful learning and faith-building experience!

Paperback / 978-1-63609-267-6